To Deborah,

my wife, my best friend, my muse!

SPSS® Plain and Simple: Analysis & Interpretation

of Group Research

Lulu Publishing
3101 Hillsborough St
Raleigh, NC 27607-5436
www.lulu.com

SPSS® is a registered trademark of IBM, Inc.

Cover Photo: *Closing time at Musée du Louvre*. 2010.
Copyright, Matthew J. Zagumny

ISBN: 978-1-105-93741-5

Copyright Matthew J. Zagumny, 2012

Printed in the United States of America

Chapter 1: SPSS® Basics

SPSS® Structure

The structure of SPSS (Statistical Package for the Social Sciences)® includes three files (See Figure 1.2): (1) a data file that always has the extension (*.sav). You'll notice that along the top of the data matrix there are gray boxes with the word 'var' in the box. These are where the variable names will be named. Variables always are listed across the top of the data file (i.e., columns) and cases are listed down the side of the data file (i.e., rows). (2) A syntax file which always has the extension(*.sps). This is our command file or if you want to talk like an engineer or computer geek you can say "this is where we are writing code." Each SPSS® command has a certain syntax or structure-the commands are very easy to write and in most cases we will just use the pull-down menus. (3) An output file which always have the extension (*.spv). This file will show us the results of the statistical analysis that we run. This file will be created by SPSS® so you don't need to worry about creating this file.

So the flow of work using SPSS®: 1) you enter the data into the data file; 2) then you write a command in the syntax file (or use the pull-down menus to generate the commands) and run the command; 3) look at the results in the viewer (output) file (which is generated for you once SPSS has calculated the results).

Naming variables

To create the data file we need to first identify which variables we will be measuring. To name a variable in SPSS®, the name must be one word (no spaces, dashes, etc.). We can use numbers in our variable names but we cannot start a variable name with a number. The first variable in our data file should be a participant number or "SUBNUM.' Why is it important to number our participants? So we can match the electronic copy of the data in SPSS® and the physical copy of the data. Online data collection systems, such as Qualtrics®, do this for us.

In all types of research, it is important to collect sociodemographic information about your participants, such as gender, race, age, etc. For the current research about the influences of religious identity, we will also need to collect other data to determine if there may be some other reason for the relationship-like maybe older people believe in heaven more than young people or females go to church more often than males. All of these are possible explanations for the influence of religious identity on other variables as well as the influence of other variables on religious identity. We will also compute, or create, new variables to categorize people who have a religion and those who do not have a religion. We will also need to recode questions from our survey instruments so that high scores on one questions represents the same as a high score on all the other questions. We will use this when we need to "reverse code" survey items that are "negatively" worded.

Variable Labels and Value Labels

The "Labels" cell in the Variable View window allows us to describe a variable name in more detail. For example, the variable name "gender" can be described as "Participant gender" to list its actually measuring.

The "Values" cell in the Variable View window allows use to place value labels on our variables to describe the codes we used for that variable. for example, if we coded the variable "gender" as 1 for female and 2 for male, we can add those values and value labels to the "gender variable in the cell headed "Values."

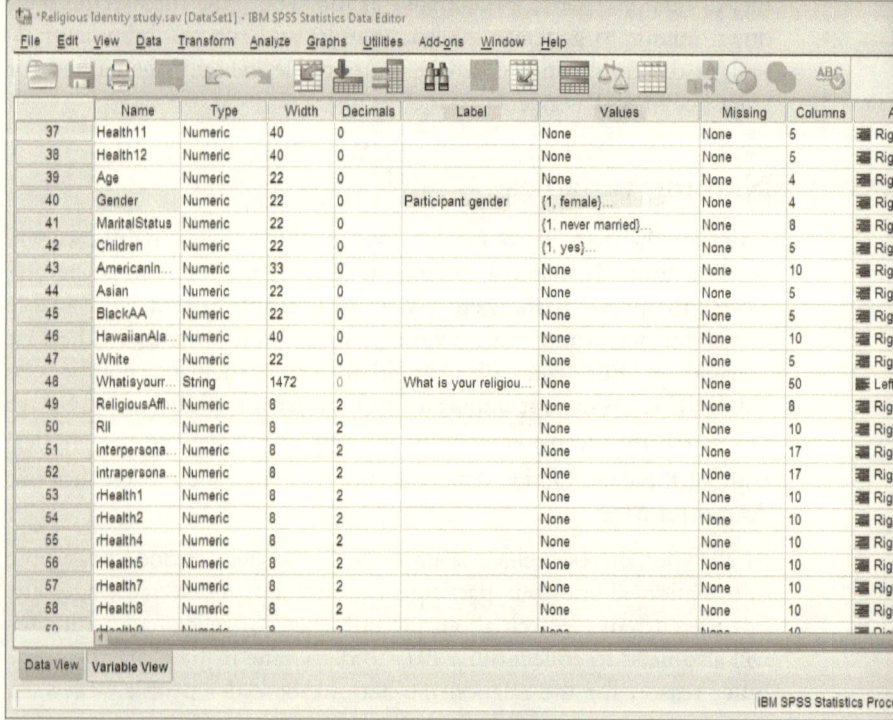

	Name	Type	Width	Decimals	Label	Values	Missing	Columns	A
37	Health11	Numeric	40	0		None	None	5	Rig
38	Health12	Numeric	40	0		None	None	5	Rig
39	Age	Numeric	22	0		None	None	4	Rig
40	Gender	Numeric	22	0	Participant gender	{1, female}...	None	4	Rig
41	MaritalStatus	Numeric	22	0		{1, never married}...	None	8	Rig
42	Children	Numeric	22	0		{1, yes}...	None	5	Rig
43	Americanin...	Numeric	33	0		None	None	10	Rig
44	Asian	Numeric	22	0		None	None	5	Rig
45	BlackAA	Numeric	22	0		None	None	5	Rig
46	HawaiianAla...	Numeric	40	0		None	None	10	Rig
47	White	Numeric	22	0		None	None	5	Rig
48	Whatisyourr...	String	1472	0	What is your religiou...	None	None	50	Left
49	ReligiousAffl...	Numeric	8	2		None	None	8	Rig
50	RII	Numeric	8	2		None	None	10	Rig
51	Interpersona...	Numeric	8	2		None	None	17	Rig
52	intrapersona...	Numeric	8	2		None	None	17	Rig
53	rHealth1	Numeric	8	2		None	None	10	Rig
54	rHealth2	Numeric	8	2		None	None	10	Rig
55	rHealth4	Numeric	8	2		None	None	10	Rig
56	rHealth5	Numeric	8	2		None	None	10	Rig
57	rHealth7	Numeric	8	2		None	None	10	Rig
58	rHealth8	Numeric	8	2		None	None	10	Rig
59	rHealth0	Numeric	8	2		None	None	10	Ri

Data View Variable View

IBM SPSS Statistics Proce

Recode Variables: Step-By-Step

a) Transform

b) Recode into Same Variable

c) Select all the variables to be recoded (make sure they are all to be recoded in the same way)

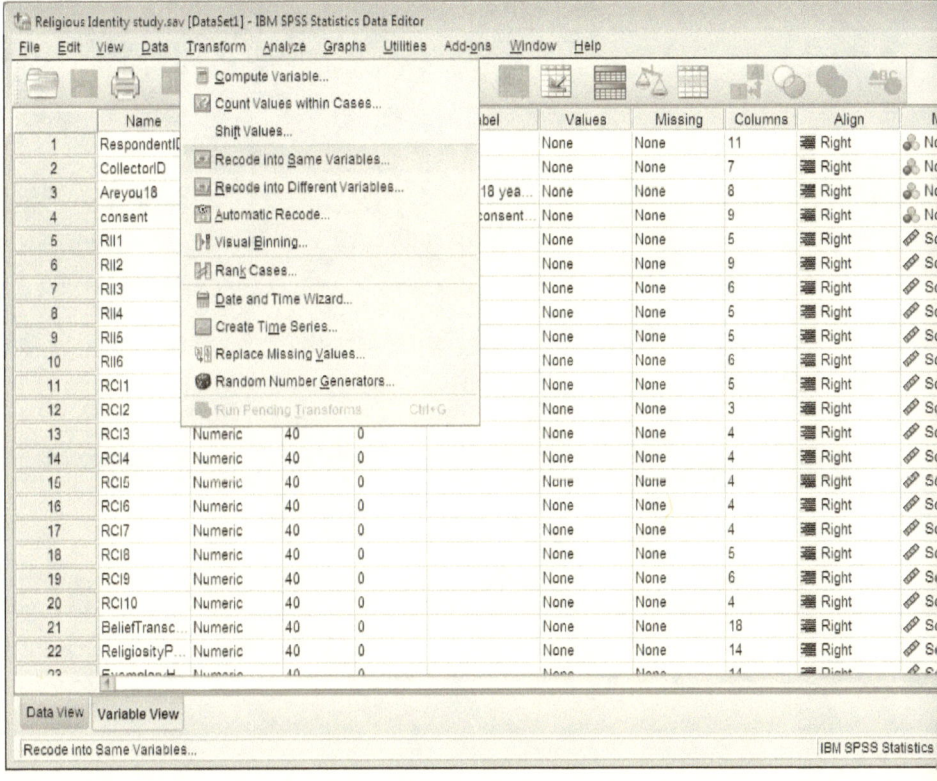

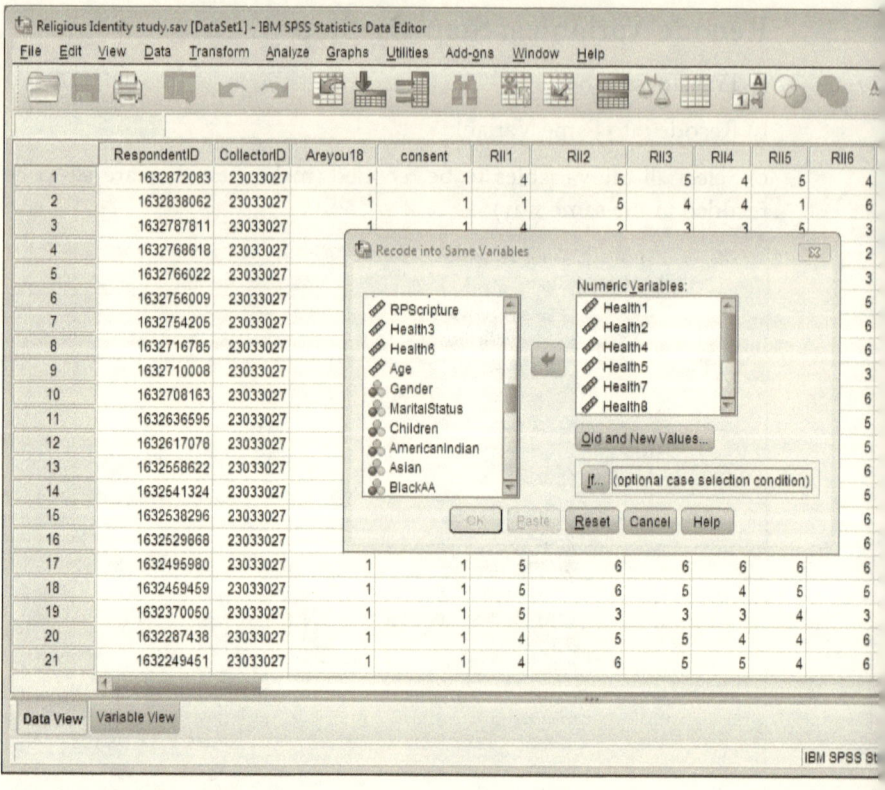

d) Old and New Values

e) Enter the old and new values - Add after each recode (Example: recoding "1" to "6," "2" to "5," etc.)

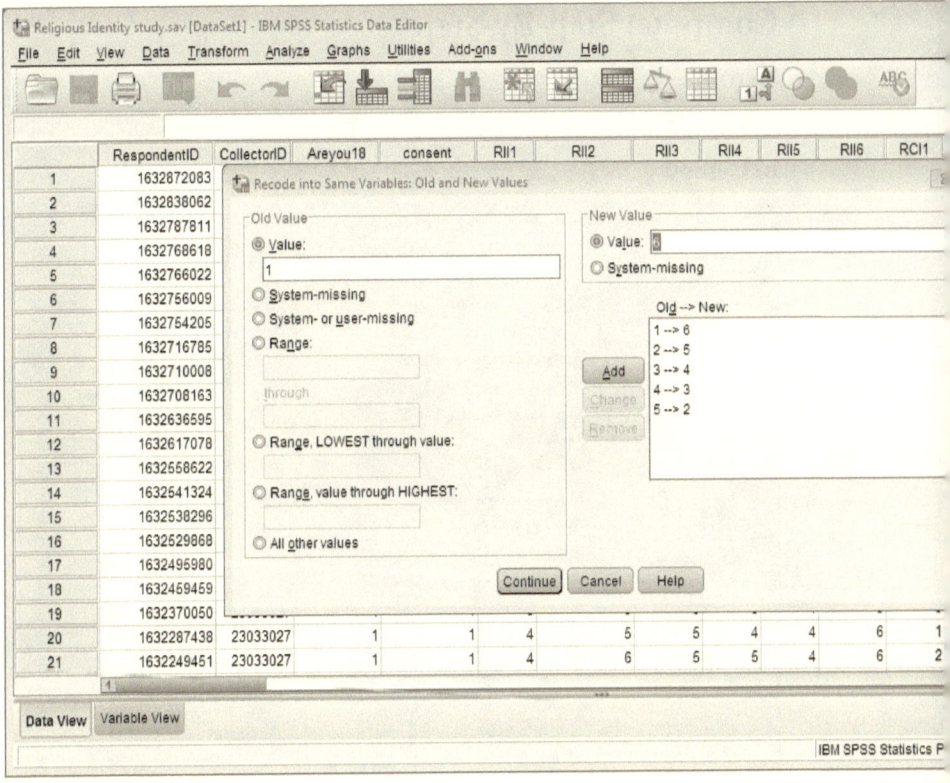

f) Continue

g) OK

Compute: Step-By-Step

Step 1:

a) Transform

b) Compute

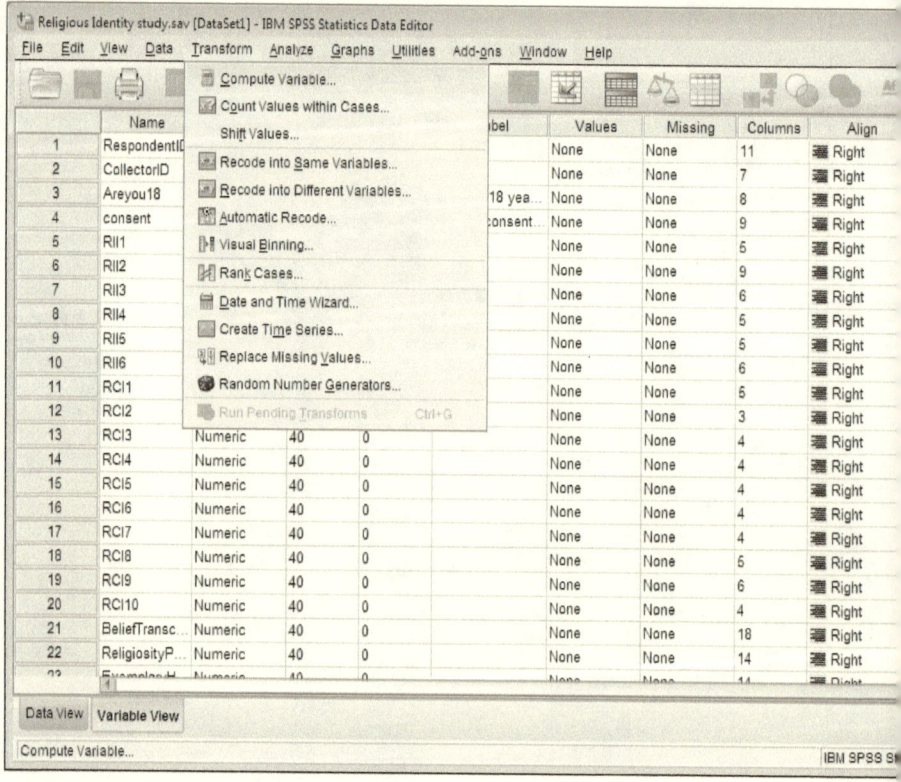

c) Type name of the new variable in "Target Variable"

d) Select "Function" for computing the new variable (Example: "Sum;" "Mean" is also common)

e) Arrow Up

f) Select variables from the list to be used to calculate/compute the new variable (make sure to separate variable names with a comma)

g) OK

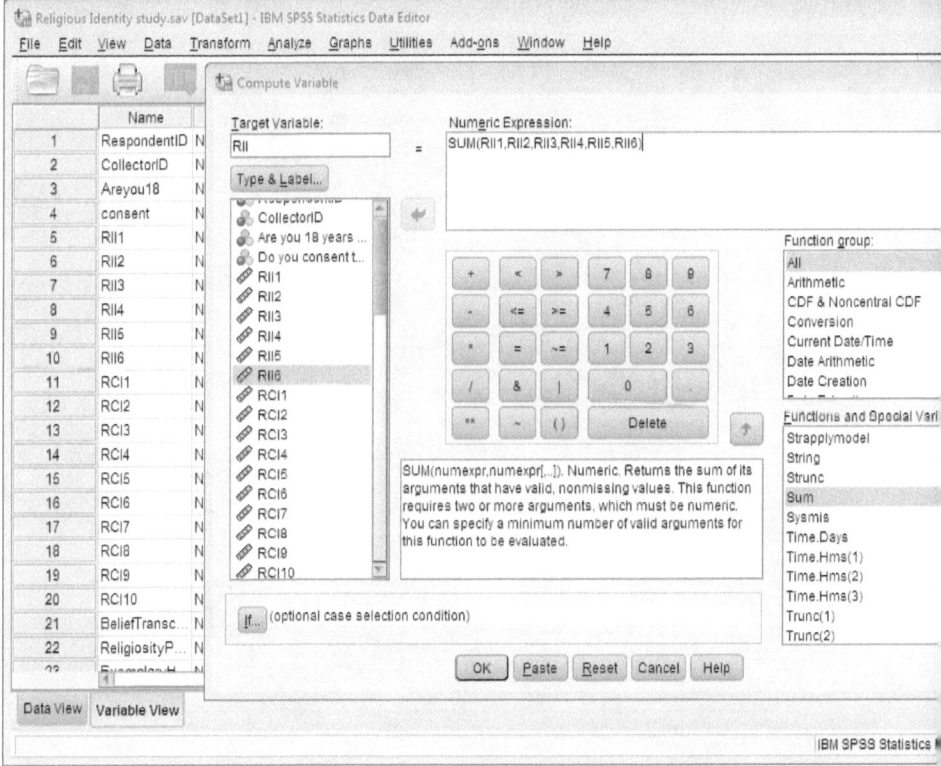

New, computed variable is listed at the end (or far right) of the data file.

Frequencies Command: Step-By-Step

Step 1:

a) Analyze

b) Descriptives Statistics

c)Frequencies

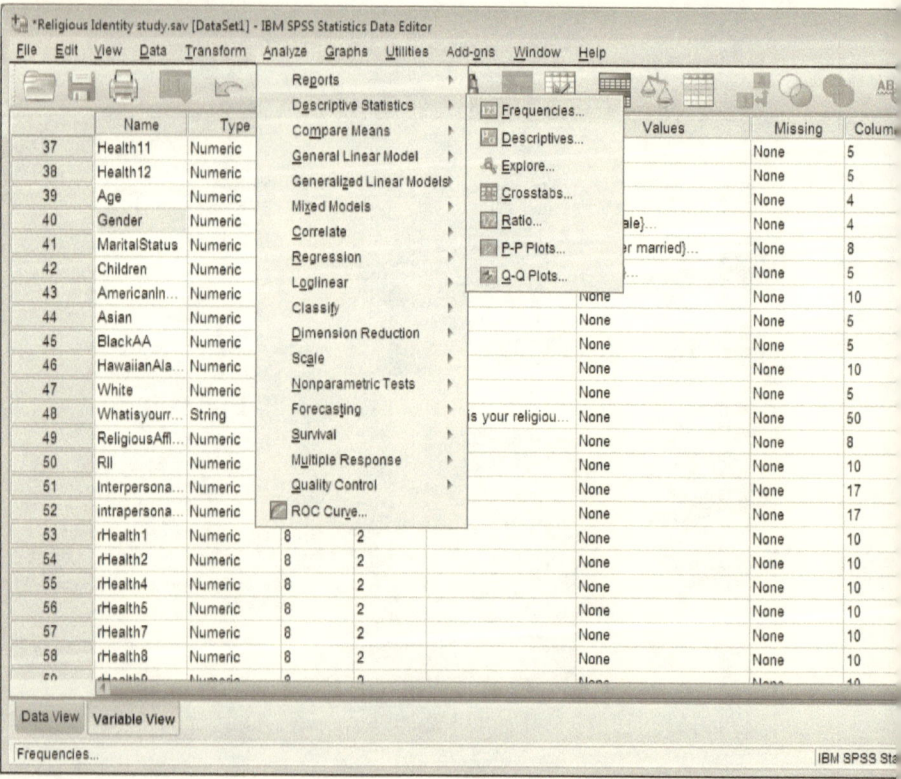

Step 2:

a) Select variables for frequencies (nominal variables)

b) OK

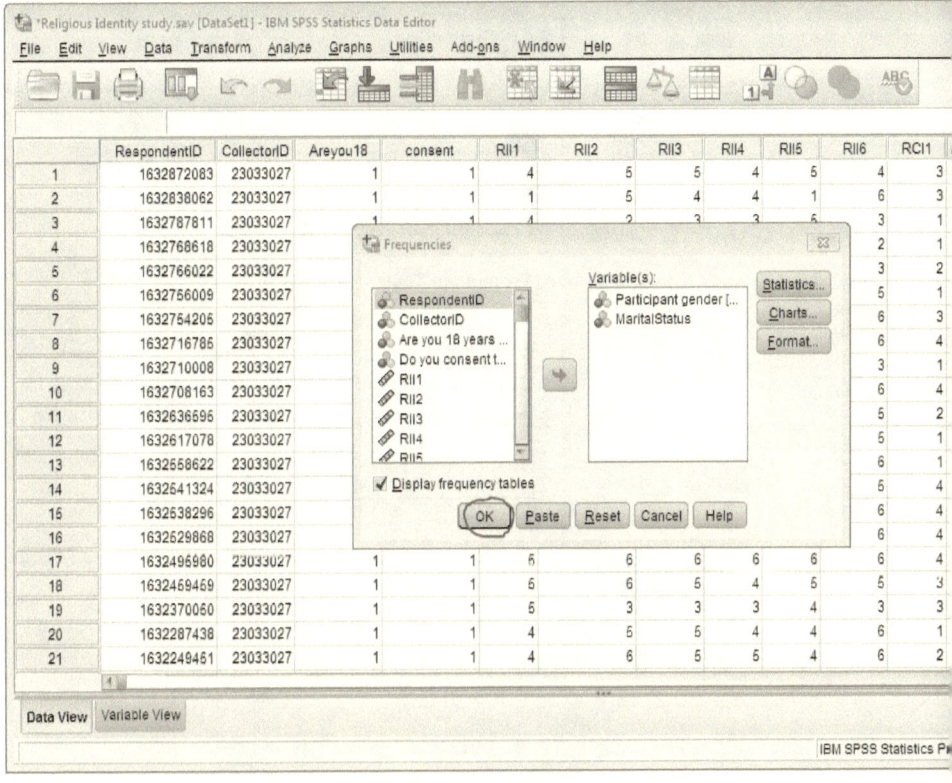

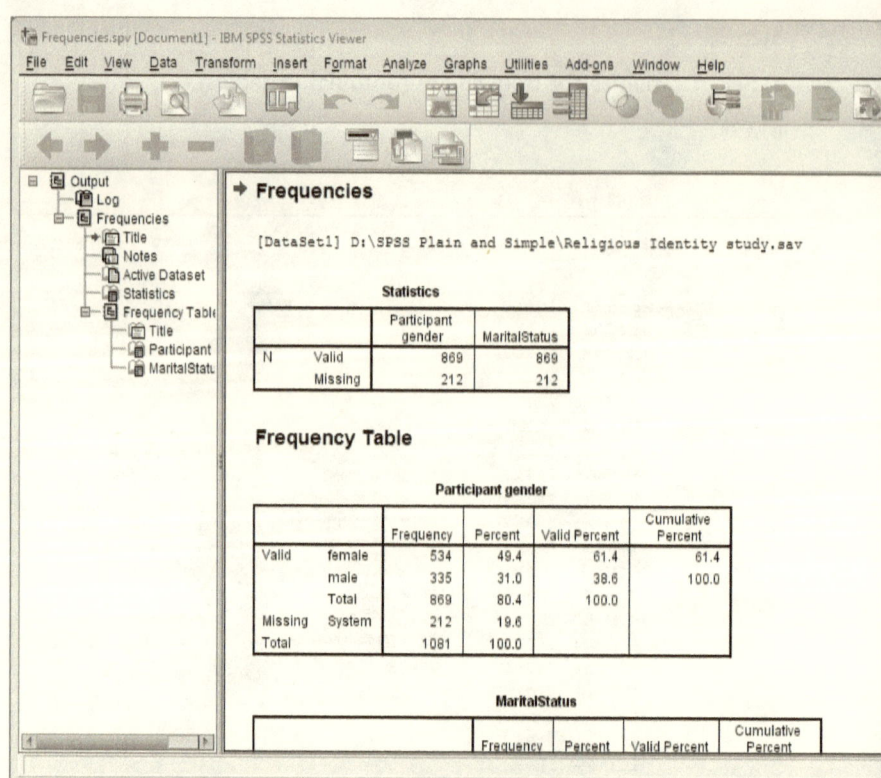

Frequencies

[DataSet1] D:\SPSS Plain and Simple\Religious Identity study.sav

Statistics

		Participant gender	MaritalStatus
N	Valid	869	869
	Missing	212	212

Frequency Table

Participant gender

		Frequency	Percent	Valid Percent	Cumulative Percent
Valid	female	534	49.4	61.4	61.4
	male	335	31.0	38.6	100.0
	Total	869	80.4	100.0	
Missing	System	212	19.6		
Total		1081	100.0		

MaritalStatus

	Frequency	Percent	Valid Percent	Cumulative Percent

Descriptives: Step-By-Step

Step 1:

a) Analyze

b) Descriptive Statistics

c) Descriptives

Step 2:

a) Options

b) Select the descriptive statistics you want from the list

c) Continue

Step 3:

a) OK

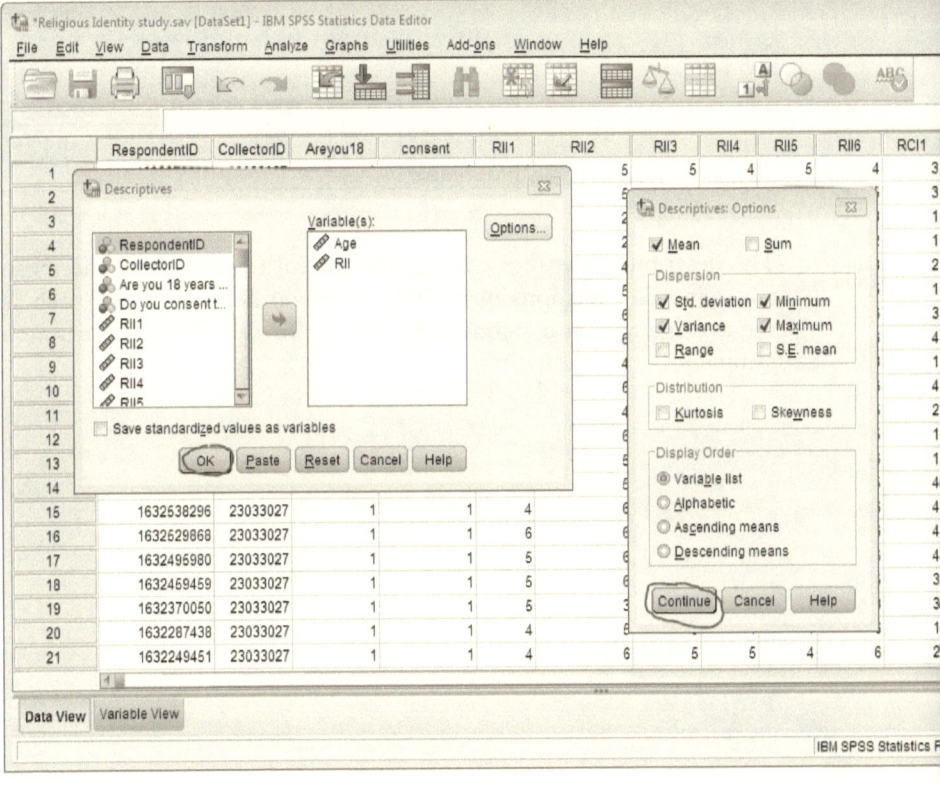

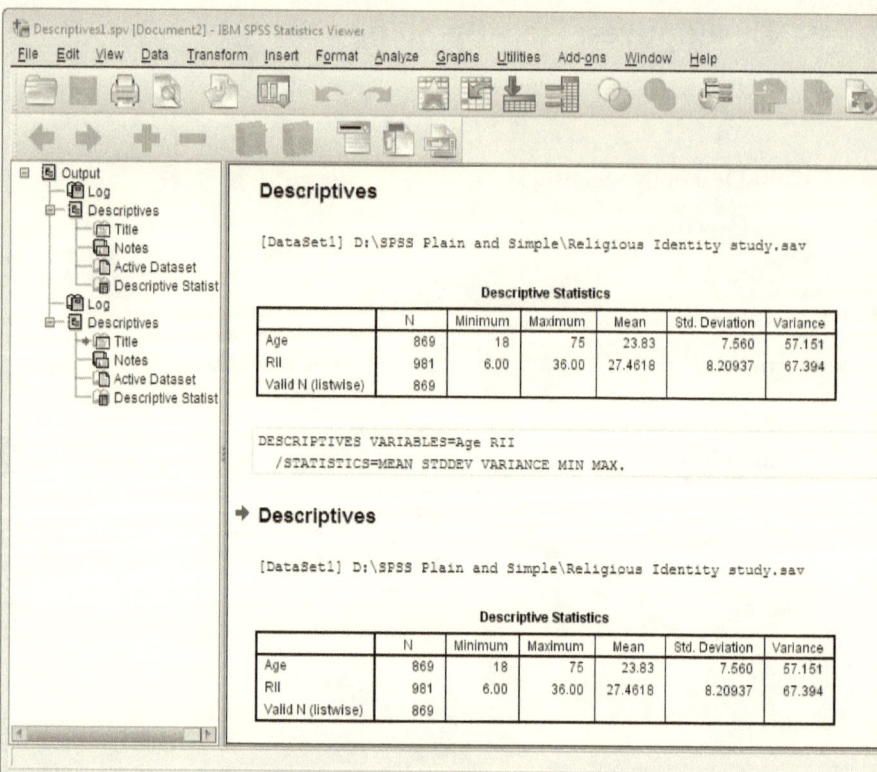

The descriptive statistics command is useful for calculated the mean and standard deviations of variables that you need to report, such as the average age (and standard deviation) for describing the research sample.

Chapter 2: t-Tests

The Independent Samples t-test is used for research designs that have two groups (or samples) that have different people in the groups (independent samples of people). The example here involves a test of those who reported themselves to have some religious tradition (labeled *Religious*) and those people who reported that they did not have a religious tradition (labeled *Nonreligious*).

Independent Samples t-Test: Step-By-Step

Step 1:

a) Analyze

b) Compare Means

c) Independent Samples t-Test

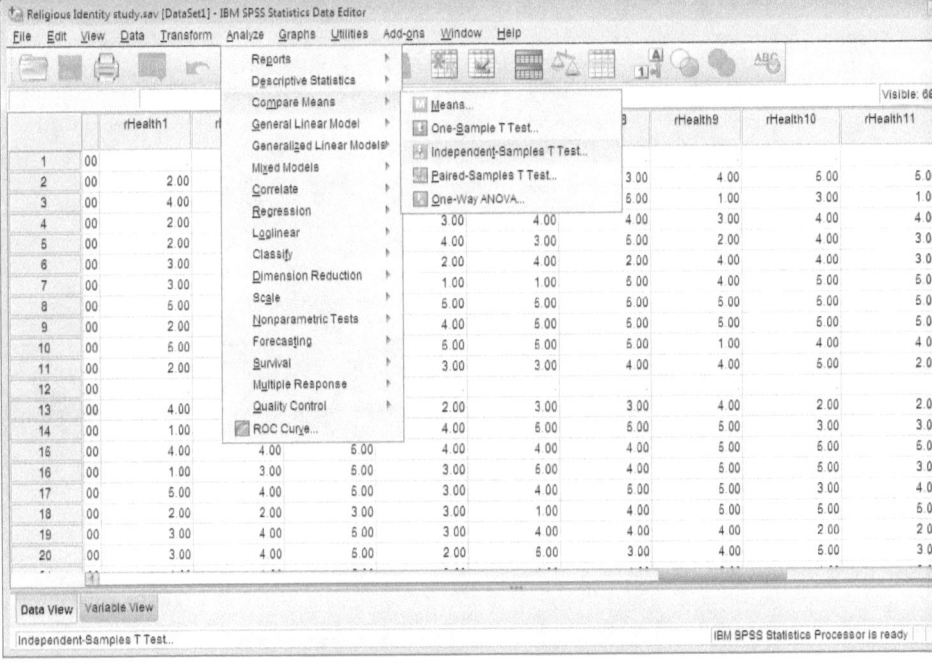

Step 2:

a) Select Dependent (Test) Variable (*RII*)

b) Select Independent (Grouping) Variable (*Affiliation1*)

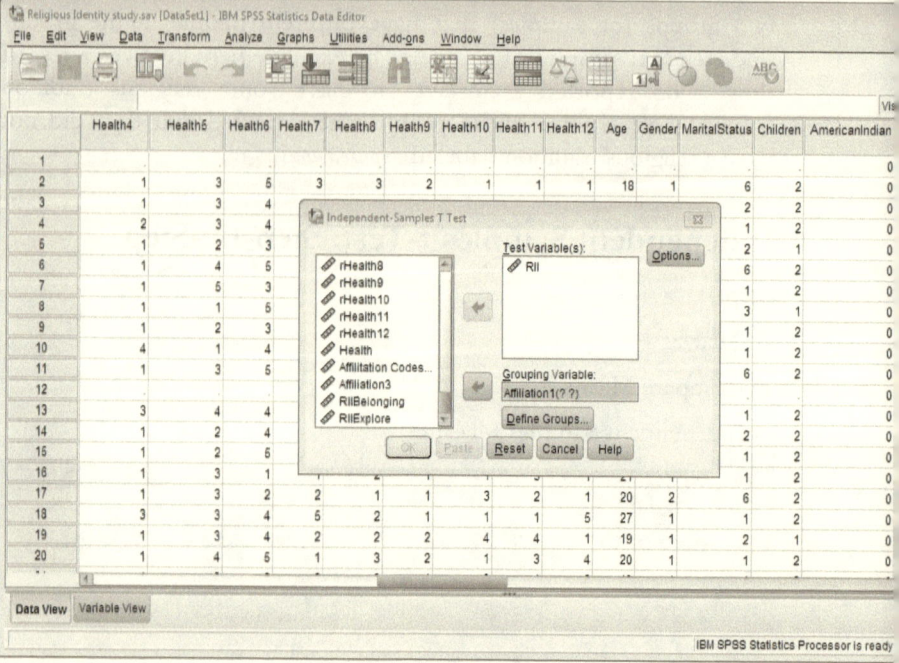

Step 3:

a) Define Groups

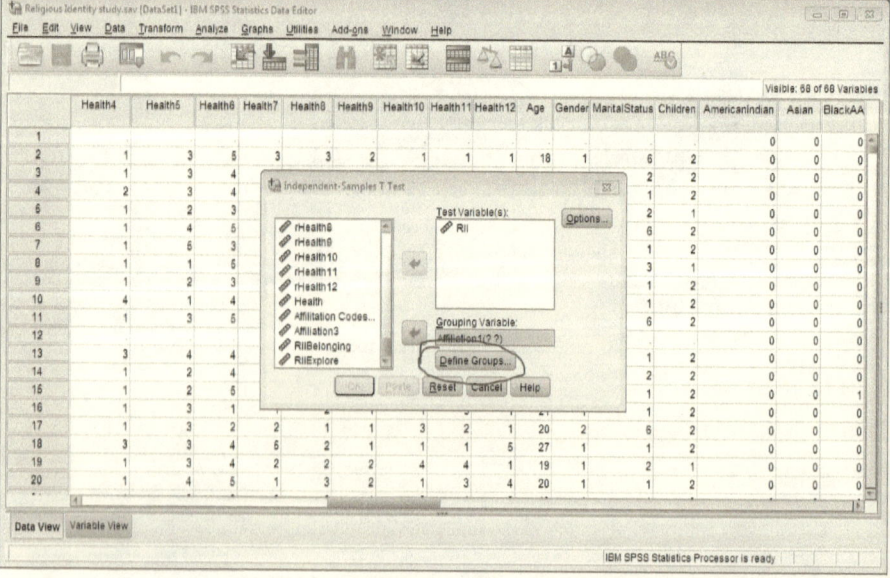

b) Enter Group 1 value code and Group 2 value code

c) Continue

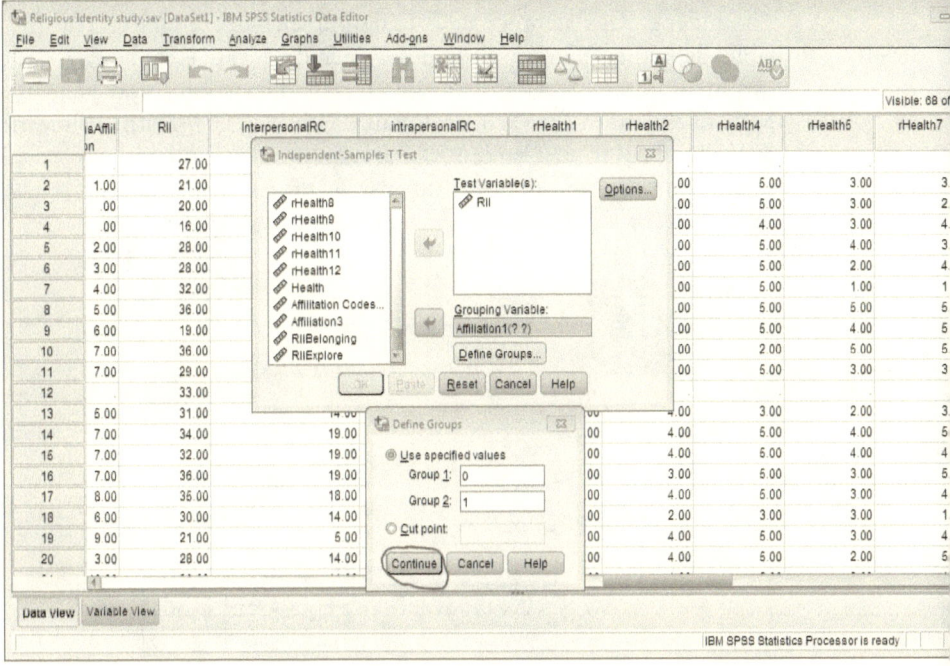

Step 4:

a) OK

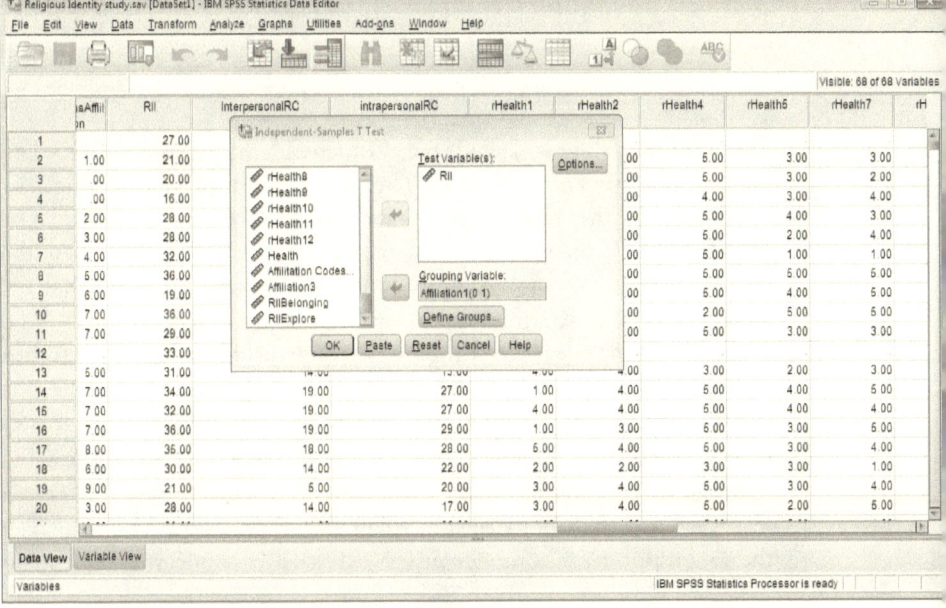

Independent Samples t-Test: Interpreting the Results

The independent samples *t* -Test output includes 2 tables. The first table lists the "Group Statistics," including the sample size (N), treatment mean, standard deviation (Std. Deviation), and standard error of the mean for each treatment condition. The treatment means will allow us to determine which of the two groups performed significantly better on the math test, *if the independent samples t - test shows that there was a significant difference between the two groups.*

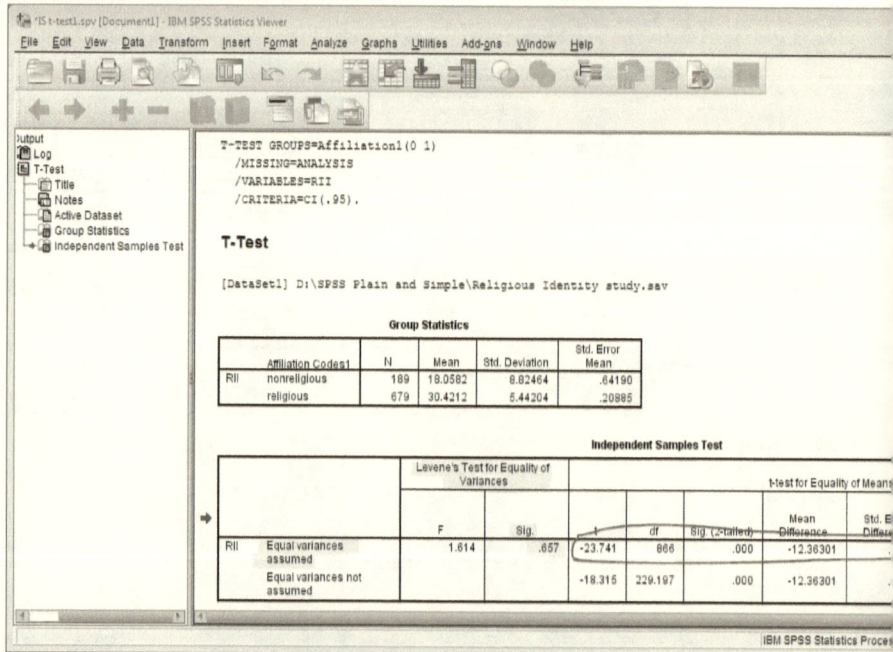

The second table is called the "Independent Samples Test" and includes two separate sections. The first section, printed on the left-hand side of the table, lists the results of "Levene's Test for the Equality of Variances" or otherwise known as a test for the homogeneity of variance assumption. This assumption states that the variances of the two treatment populations are equal: $\sigma_1^2 = \sigma_2^2$. To evaluate Levene's test we compare the value listed under "Sig." to our alpha level (.05 or .01, whichever you are using). In our example, the significance level reported under Levene's test is .788 which is greater than our α=.01, therefore, we did not brake the assumption of homogeneity of variances. If the "Sig." value listed under Levene's test were less than our decision rule (α=.01), we would have broken the assumption of homogeneity. Next we'll examine the right-hand

18

side of the second table in the output; the "$\underline{t}$ - test for Equality of Means."

Since we did not break the assumption of homogeneity in our example, we will interpret the top row of the "Equality of Means" table. This top row is headed "Equal variances assumed." This portion of the table lists the $\underline{t}$ value, degrees of freedom (df = n_1 + n_2 -2), the significance level of $\underline{t}$ - test (Sig. 2-tailed), mean difference ($\underline{M_1}$ - $\underline{M_2}$), the standard error of the difference (Std. Error Difference: $S_{x1\text{-}x2}$), and the confidence intervals for the differences between the treatment means with "Lower" and "Upper" confidence intervals.

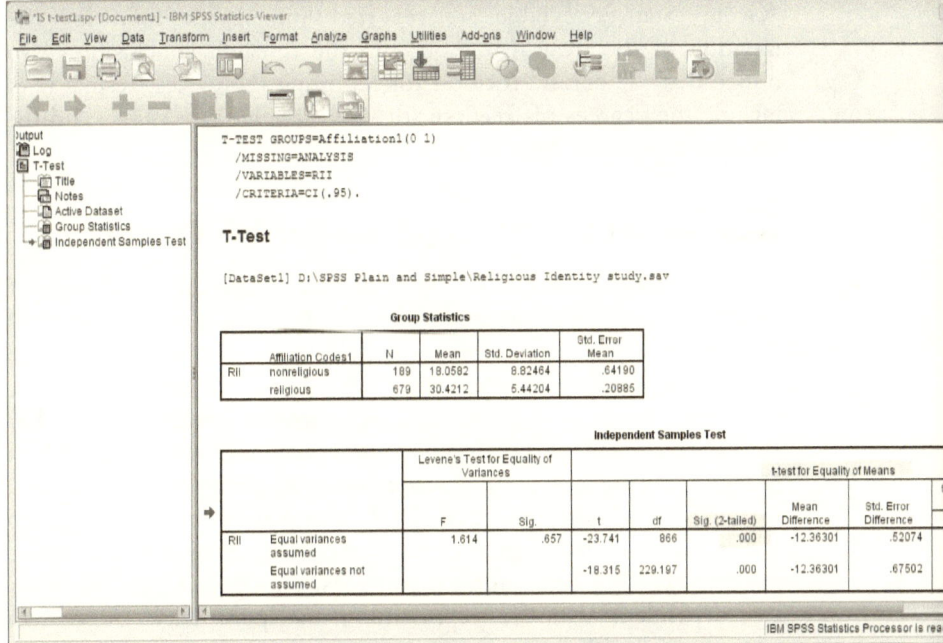

To evaluate the significance of the $\underline{t}$ - test we compare the significance level reported under "Sig. (2-tailed)" with our decision rule (α=.01). For our music example, the calculated significance level was .000, which is interpreted as .001. Since the calculated significance level is less than the decision rule of .01, we would reject the null (H_0) and conclude that there is a significant difference between the two treatment populations. Remember that the null hypothesis states the two treatment population means are equal (i.e. μ_1 = μ_2). Since we rejected the null hypothesis, we are concluding that $\mu_1 \neq \mu_2$. We now examine the treatment means and see that those students who reported that they were "religious" had a significantly higher score on the RII than those students who reported that they were "nonreligious."

Independent Samples t-Test: Reporting the Results

Since we found a significant t - test result we would report the findings as follow:

Those students who reported they were religious (M = 30.42, SD = 5.44) scored significantly higher on religious identity than those who reported themselves to be nonreligious (M = 18.06, SD = 8.82) while studying, t (866) = 1-23.74, p < .001.

Notice that the means (M) and standard deviations (SD) from the "Group Statistics" table are reported immediately following the mention of the treatment groups in the research conclusion. Also notice that the correct method for reporting the t - test results is to include the degrees of freedom (df=866), t value (t=-23.74), and the calculated significance level (p < .001).

Independent Samples t-Test: Further Practice

You are researchers interested in examining the effect of type of music on math performance. Specifically, you are interested in whether classical music improves college students' performance on a math test. You decide to use a two group design with people randomly assigned to either an experimental condition that has students listening to U2 (rock treatment condition) or to Mozart (classical treatment group). You randomly assign 28 students to each treatment condition for a total N=56. The participants in each group will listen to their assigned music while completing a test on basic mathematics. We'll measure the math test on a percentage scale with the dependent measure representing the percentage of correct responses (0%-100%).

SUBNUM	MUSIC	GRADE
1.00	1.00	47.00
2.00	1.00	43.00
3.00	1.00	39.00
4.00	1.00	53.00
5.00	1.00	42.00
6.00	1.00	56.00
7.00	1.00	53.00
8.00	1.00	52.00
9.00	1.00	46.00
10.00	1.00	45.00
11.00	1.00	44.00
12.00	1.00	53.00

13.00	1.00	39.00
14.00	1.00	53.00
15.00	1.00	62.00
16.00	1.00	45.00
17.00	1.00	56.00
18.00	1.00	41.00
19.00	1.00	46.00
20.00	1.00	48.00
21.00	1.00	57.00
22.00	1.00	54.00
23.00	1.00	45.00
24.00	1.00	51.00
25.00	1.00	62.00
26.00	1.00	44.00
27.00	1.00	55.00
28.00	1.00	38.00
29.00	2.00	72.00
30.00	2.00	77.00
31.00	2.00	90.00
32.00	2.00	88.00
33.00	2.00	80.00
34.00	2.00	82.00
35.00	2.00	85.00
36.00	2.00	74.00
37.00	2.00	93.00
38.00	2.00	86.00
39.00	2.00	93.00
40.00	2.00	86.00
41.00	2.00	96.00
42.00	2.00	77.00
43.00	2.00	88.00
44.00	2.00	72.00
45.00	2.00	90.00
46.00	2.00	90.00
47.00	2.00	94.00
48.00	2.00	71.00
49.00	2.00	97.00
50.00	2.00	97.00
51.00	2.00	82.00
52.00	2.00	87.00
53.00	2.00	85.00
54.00	2.00	83.00
55.00	2.00	81.00
56.00	2.00	78.00

Paired-Samples t-Test: Step-By-Step

The Paired-Sample t-test is used for two research designs:

1) pretest-posttest designs

2) matched (or repeated measures) designs

In our research study we asked people to rate their level of religious identity along two related dimensions: 1) a sense of belonging to their religion and 2) the desire to explore their religion. These dimensions are named *RIIBelong* and *RIIExplore*. To determine if the same person scored differently on these two dimensions we can conduct a paired-samples t-test.

Step 1:

a) Analyze

b) Compare Means

c) Paired-Samples t-Test

Step 2:

a) Select first measurement (*RIIBelong*) and then second measurement (*RIIExplore*)

Step 3:

a) OK

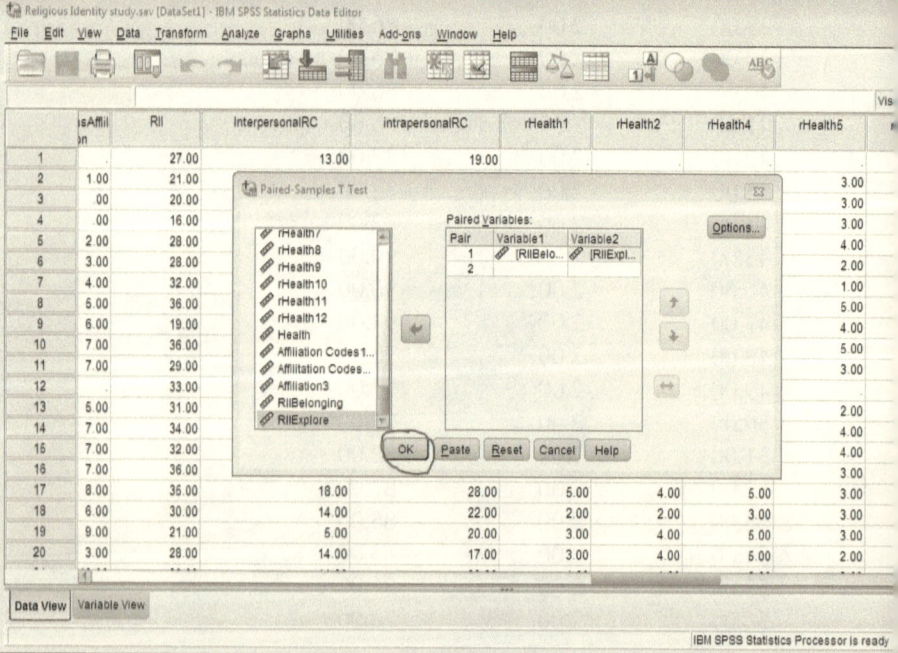

Paired-Samples t-Test: Interpreting the Results

We again look at the Sig. (2-tailed) probability on the output to determine if the test was significant. Again, when the Sig. (2-talied) value is less than our decision rule the difference between the two measures is significant.

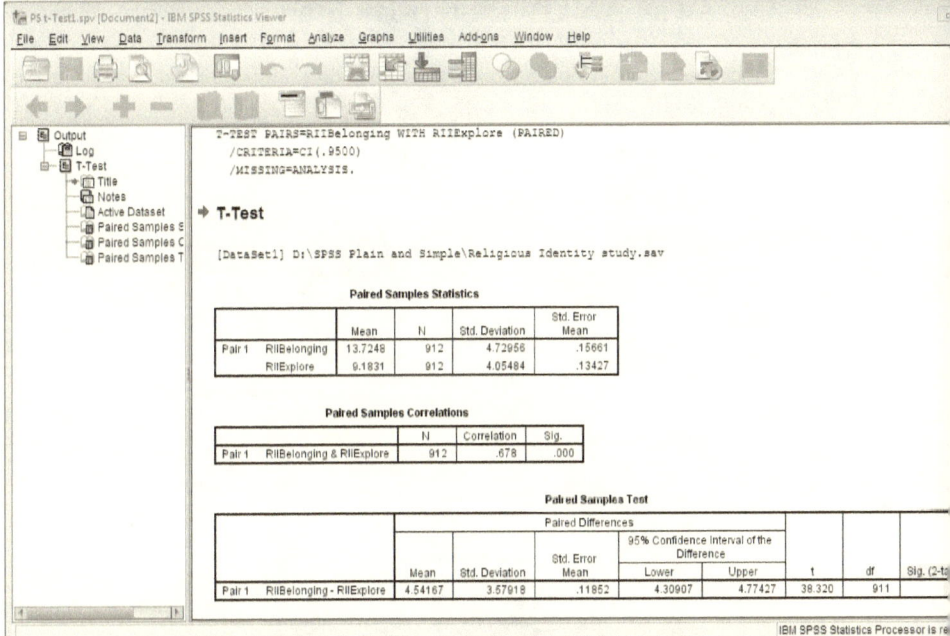

For the example the Sig.(2-tailed) (.001) < decision rule (.01) so the finding is statistically significant. We look at the means for each measure (in the Paired Sample Statistics table) to determine which score was significantly higher. In the example *RIIBelong* had a mean of 13.72 and *RIIExplore* had a mean of 9.18.

Paired-Samples t-Test: Reporting the Results

Participants' sense of religious identity was significantly higher in their sense of "belonging" ($M = 13.74$, $SD = 4.73$) compared to their sense of "exploration" ($M = 9.18$, $SD = 4.05$), t (911) = 38.32, $p < .001$.

Chapter 3: One-Way Analysis of Variance (ANOVA)

One-Way ANOVA: Step-By-Step

Step 1:

a) Analyze

b) Compare Means

c) One-Way ANOVA

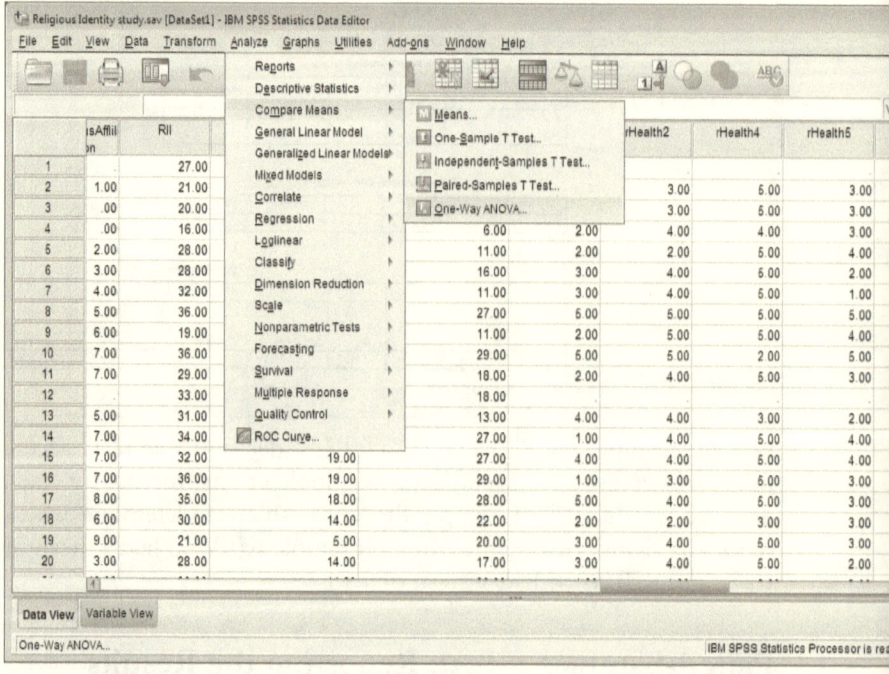

Step 2:

a) Select Dependent Variable (*RII)*

b) Select Independent (Factor) Variable (*Affiliation Codes 2)*

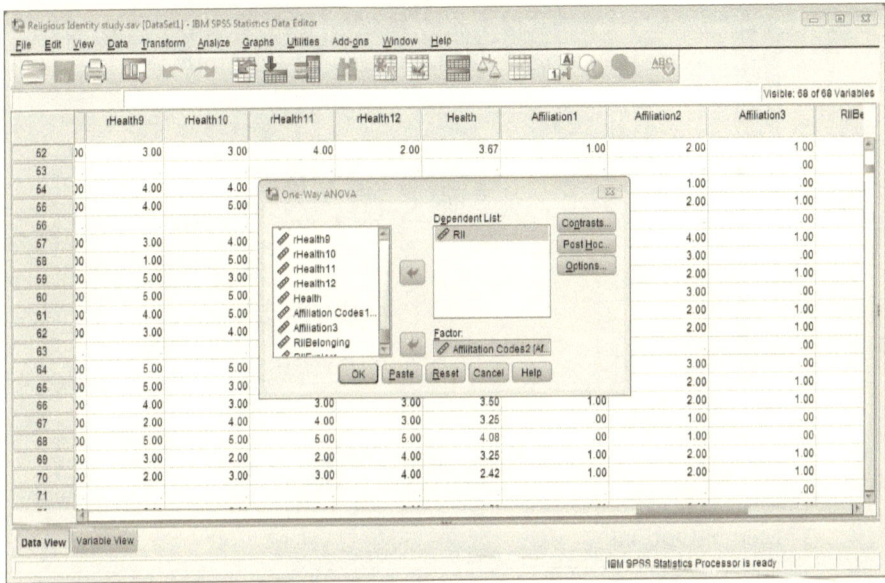

Step 3: Post Hoc

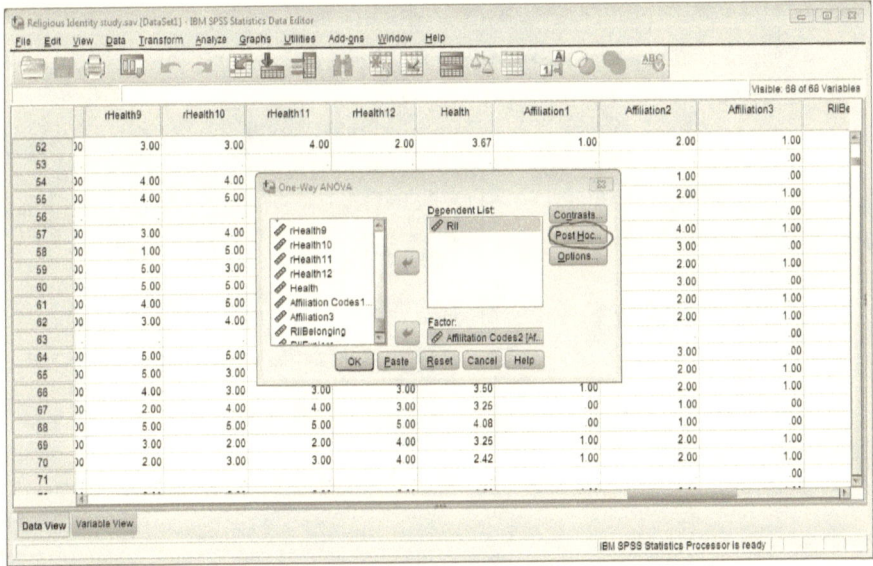

25

Step 4: LSD (or other multiple comparison tests)

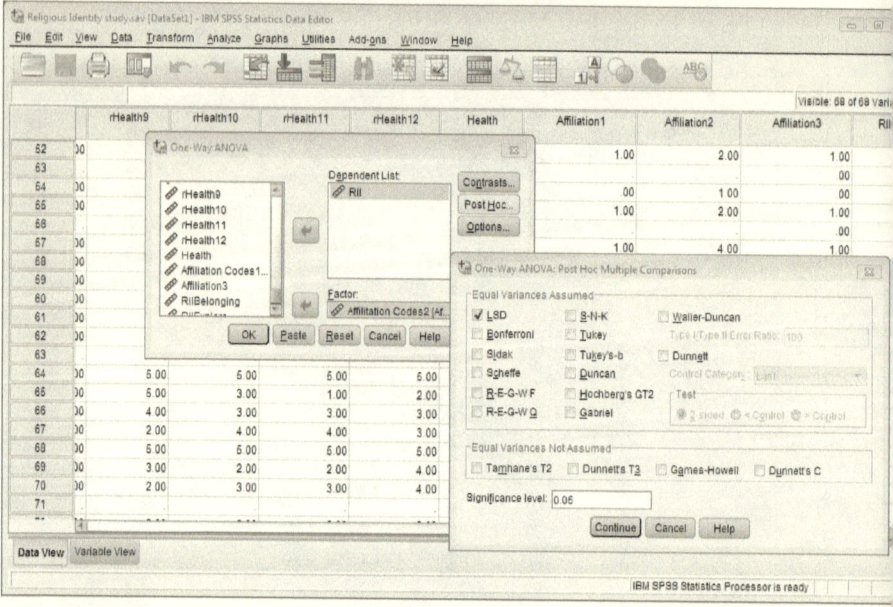

Step 5: Options

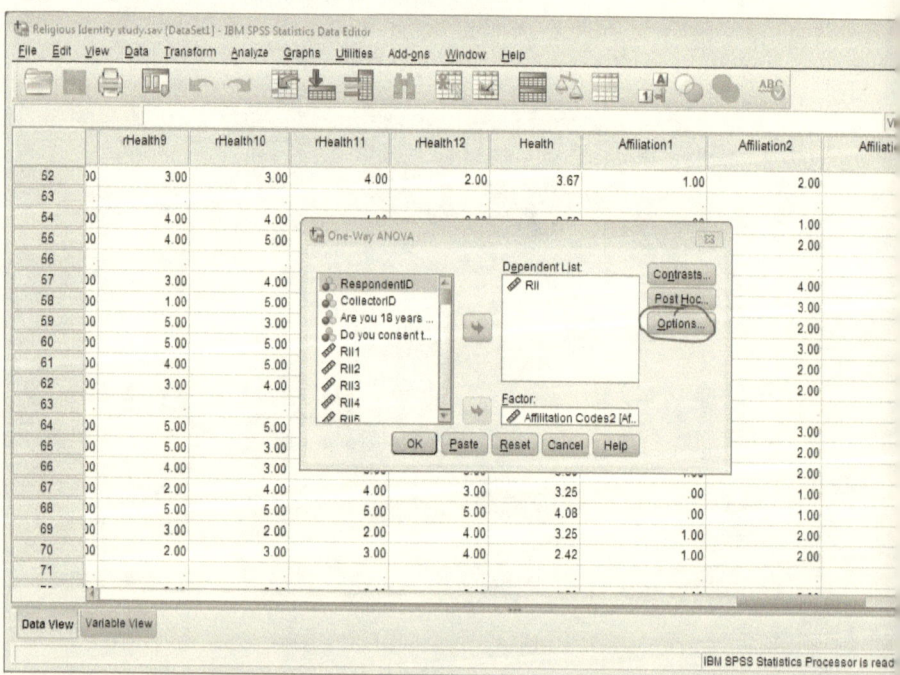

Step 6: Descriptives

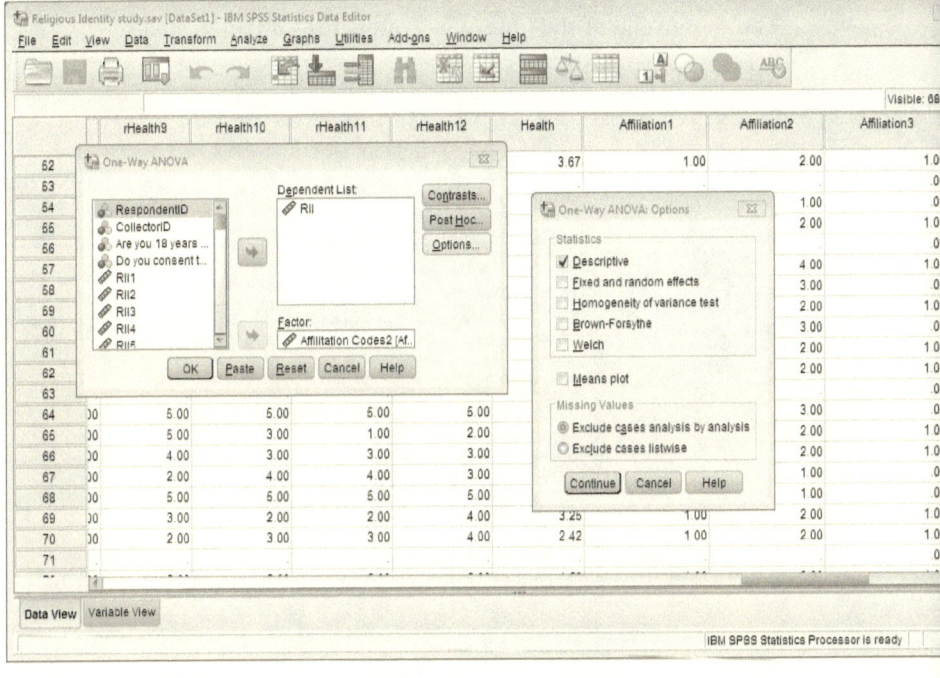

One-Way ANOVA: Interpreting the Results

The output file of the One-Way command lists three tables.

1. Descriptives table

2. ANOVA table

3. Multiple Comparisons table

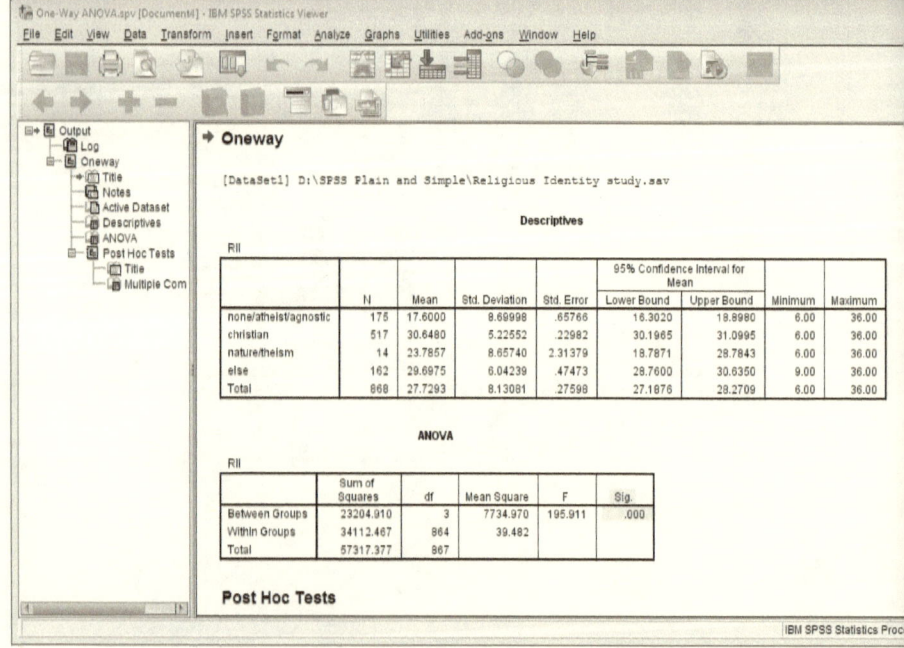

Descriptives Table

The first table is the One-Way descriptives table. This table lists the means and standard deviations of each treatment condition in the research design. This information is important because when you report the results of the One-way research design in a research report, you must include the mean and standard deviation of each treatment group, regardless of whether there were significant differences between the groups or not.

ANOVA (Source) Table

The next table listed in the One-Way ANOVA printout is called the ANOVA *source table*. This lists the sources of variation as *between groups (or treatment variance)*, *within groups (or error variance)*, and *total variance*. The sum of squares, degrees of freedom (df), mean squares, F statistic, and the significance level of the F statistic. To evaluate the statistical significance of this F statistic we examine the "Sig." value printed in the source table. The "Sig." value listed is .000, which we interpret as $p < .001$. Since this is less than our decision rule of α=.01, we would "Reject the H_0" and conclude that there is a significant difference between at least two of the treatment population means.

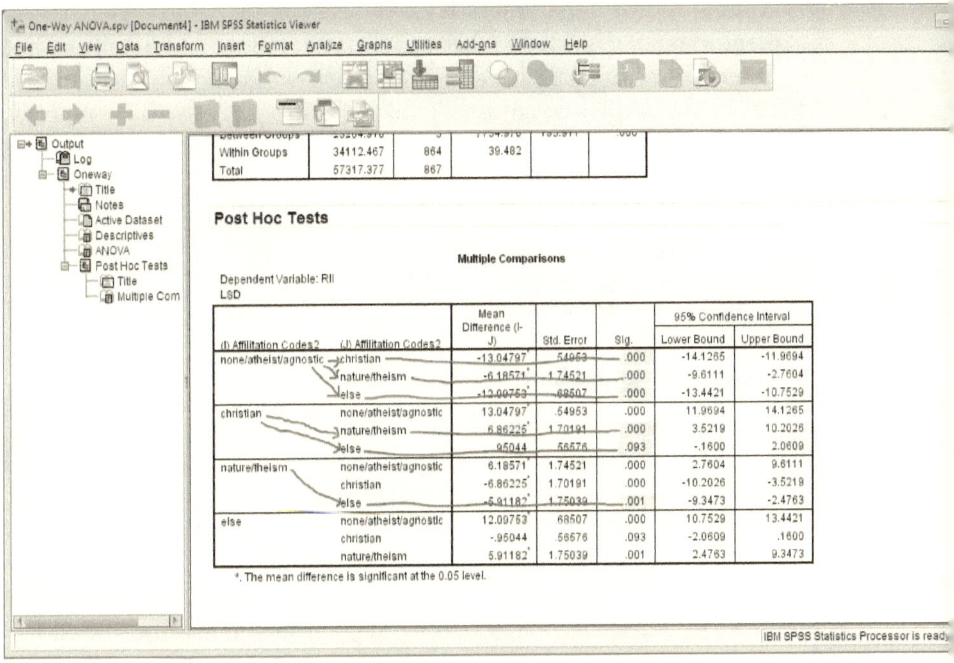

[illegible]					
Within Groups	34112.467	864	39.482		
Total	57317.377	867			

Post Hoc Tests

Multiple Comparisons

Dependent Variable: RII
LSD

(I) Affiliation Codes2	(J) Affiliation Codes2	Mean Difference (I-J)	Std. Error	Sig.	95% Confidence Interval Lower Bound	Upper Bound
none/atheist/agnostic	christian	-13.04797*	.54953	.000	-14.1265	-11.9694
	nature/theism	-6.18571*	1.74521	.000	-9.6111	-2.7604
	else	-12.09753*	.68507	.000	-13.4421	-10.7529
christian	none/atheist/agnostic	13.04797*	.54953	.000	11.9694	14.1265
	nature/theism	6.86225*	1.70191	.000	3.5219	10.2026
	else	.95044	.56576	.093	-.1600	2.0609
nature/theism	none/atheist/agnostic	6.18571*	1.74521	.000	2.7604	9.6111
	christian	-6.86225*	1.70191	.000	-10.2026	-3.5219
	else	-5.91182*	1.75039	.001	-9.3473	-2.4763
else	none/atheist/agnostic	12.09753*	.68507	.000	10.7529	13.4421
	christian	-.95044	.56576	.093	-2.0609	.1600
	nature/theism	5.91182*	1.75039	.001	2.4763	9.3473

*. The mean difference is significant at the 0.05 level.

Post Hoc Multiple Comparison Tests

The next step is to evaluate the *post hoc* multiple comparison test results to determine which means are significantly different from each other. SPSS lists all of the possible pairwise (or two group) comparisons twice. Each treatment group is listed under group "I" and "J" in the multiple comparisons table. SPSS calculates the "Mean Difference" listed in this table by taking the treatment mean of the first group (group "I") and subtracting the treatment mean of the second group (group "J"). To determine if the comparison is statistically significant, we compare the "Sig." level listed for each unique *post hoc* test to our decision rule (α=.01). As we examine the multiple comparisons table we see that 5 of the 6 comparisons between the four different religious affiliation codes (*None/Atheist/Agnostic, Christian, Nature/Theism* and *Else*) are significant (the 5 significant comparisons have a Sig. < .001, which we interpret as .001). Now we examine the treatment group means listed in the Descriptives table to determine which group reported higher *RII* (Religious Identity Index) scores.

One-Way ANOVA: Reporting the Results

When you report the F statistic and/or the multiple comparisons, it should take the following format. This would be reported in the Results section of an APA style research manuscript:

Results of the One-Way ANOVA showed that the overall $\underline{F}$ was significant, $\underline{F}$ (3,864) = 195.91, MS_E = 39.48, $\underline{p}$ < .001. Post hoc comparisons using Fisher's LSD test, relieved that people categorized as "None/Atheist/Agnostic" (M = 17.6, SD = 8.7) reported significantly less religious identity than those categorized as "Christians" (M = 30.65, SD = 5.23), "Nature/Theism" (M = 23.79, SD = 8.66) and "Else" (M = 29.7, SD = 6.04). Additionally, those categorized as "Nature/Theism" reported significantly less religious identity than those categorized as "Christians" or "Else." All other comparisons were nonsignificant.

Important note about *Post Hoc* tests!

Remember that we only evaluate the *post hoc* multiple comparison when the overall $\underline{F}$ statistic is significant (i.e., has a Sig. equal to or less than .01). If we evaluated the multiple comparisons after determining that the overall $\underline{F}$ statistic was nonsignificant, we run the risk of committing a Type I Error. If the overall $\underline{F}$ statistic was nonsignificant that would mean that we Failed to Reject the H_0 that states $\mu_1 = \mu_2 = \mu_3 = \mu_4$. So, if we are concluding that the null should not be rejected, there is no reason to continue to conduct statistical testing on the same data. When we make the statistical decision of "Fail to Reject H_0" we are concluding that the population means are equal, so we don't go searching for significant differences between pairs of treatment means.

One-Way ANOVA: Further Practice

Let's study the effects of alcohol on driving ability. We design a study that involves three (3) levels of ALCOHOL CONSUMPTION (the independent variable): (1) No alcohol; (2) 24 oz of beer; and (3) 48 oz of beer consumed in 60 minutes. The dependent variable will be DRIVING ABILITY, which we can measure on a closed-circuit driving course that uses orange construction cones as the course boundaries. The dependent variable will be measured as the number of cones hit by the driver, so lower dependent variable values represent better driving ability and higher values represent worse driving ability. Using the following data, conduct the One-way ANOVA and write up the results section of an APA manuscript based on your analysis.

SUBNUM	ALCOHOL	DRIVING
1.00	1.00	6.00
2.00	1.00	9.00
3.00	1.00	10.00
4.00	1.00	7.00
5.00	1.00	8.00
6.00	1.00	6.00
7.00	1.00	8.00
8.00	1.00	9.00
9.00	1.00	6.00
10.00	1.00	9.00
11.00	1.00	7.00
12.00	1.00	8.00
13.00	1.00	9.00
14.00	1.00	6.00
15.00	1.00	7.00
16.00	1.00	7.00
17.00	1.00	7.00
18.00	1.00	8.00
19.00	1.00	7.00
20.00	1.00	9.00
21.00	2.00	3.00
22.00	2.00	4.00
23.00	2.00	3.00
24.00	2.00	2.00
25.00	2.00	3.00
26.00	2.00	7.00
27.00	2.00	2.00
28.00	2.00	3.00
29.00	2.00	5.00
30.00	2.00	2.00
31.00	2.00	3.00
32.00	2.00	5.00
33.00	2.00	3.00
34.00	2.00	4.00
35.00	2.00	4.00
36.00	2.00	3.00
37.00	2.00	2.00
38.00	2.00	6.00
39.00	2.00	7.00
40.00	2.00	2.00
41.00	3.00	3.00
42.00	3.00	5.00
43.00	3.00	4.00
44.00	3.00	5.00

45.00	3.00	3.00
46.00	3.00	4.00
47.00	3.00	6.00
48.00	3.00	5.00
49.00	3.00	5.00
50.00	3.00	5.00
51.00	3.00	6.00
52.00	3.00	7.00
53.00	3.00	5.00
54.00	3.00	6.00
55.00	3.00	5.00
56.00	3.00	3.00
57.00	3.00	5.00
58.00	3.00	2.00
59.00	3.00	4.00
60.00	3.00	4.00

Chapter 4: Factorial Analysis of Variance (ANOVA)

In this analysis we use two factors (or independent variables):

1) *Affiliation1* which is coded as 0=nonreligious and 1=religious

2) *Gender* coded as 1=females and 2=males

and *RII* (religious identity scores) as the dependent variable

Factorial ANOVA: Step-By-Step

Step 1:

a) File

b) New

c) Syntax

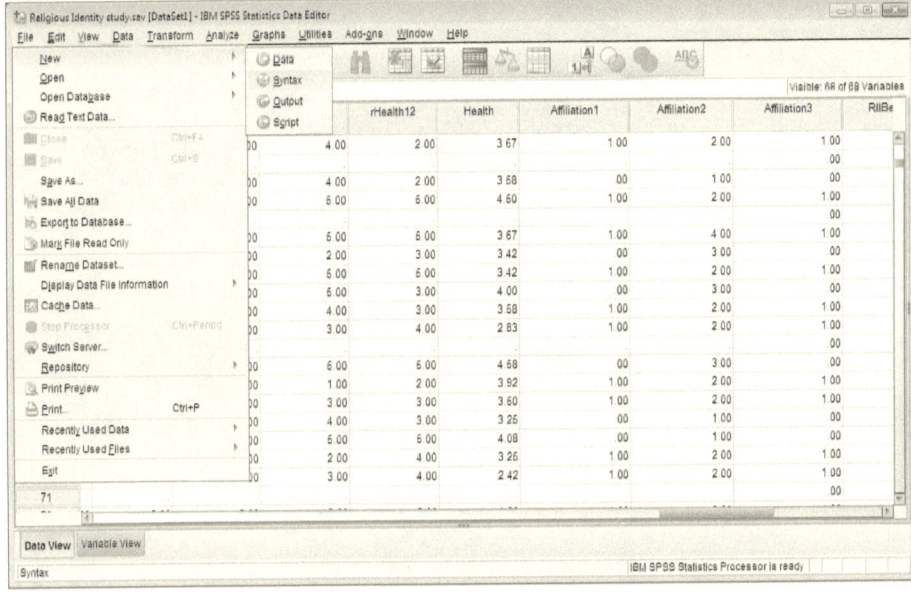

Step 2: Type MANOVA command for factorial ANOVA

a) MANOVA *dv name* BY *factor1 name*(*min, max*) *factor2 name* (*min, max*)
   /PRINT SIGNIF (AVONLY)
   /OMEANS.
b) Run (Green Arrow Button in next screenshot)

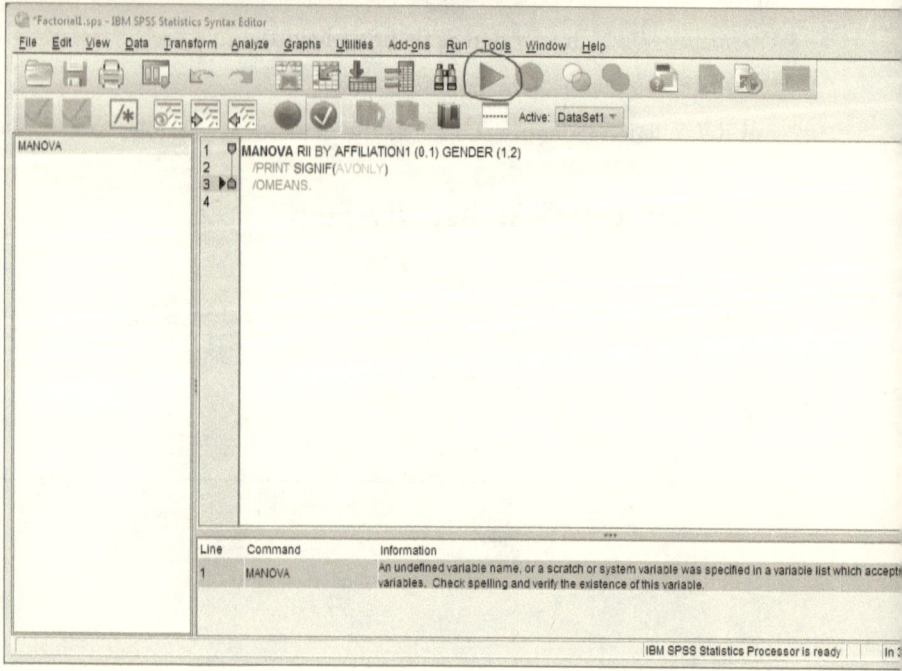

Factorial ANOVA: Interpreting the Results

The output contains two tables:

1) Means, Standard Deviations, N (sample size) table

2) ANOVA (Source) table

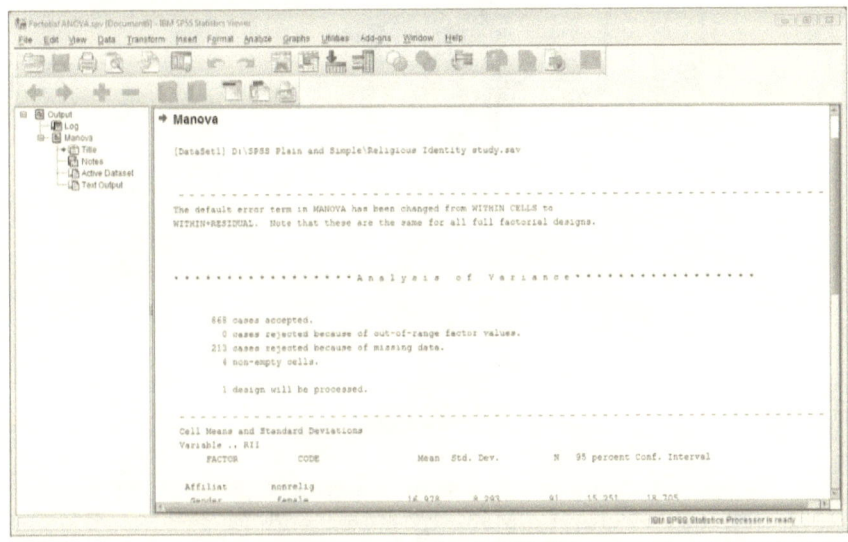

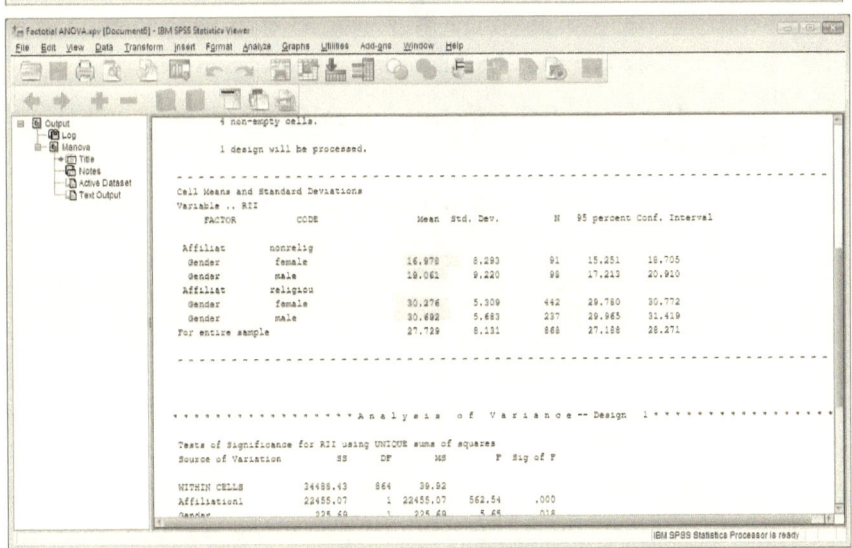

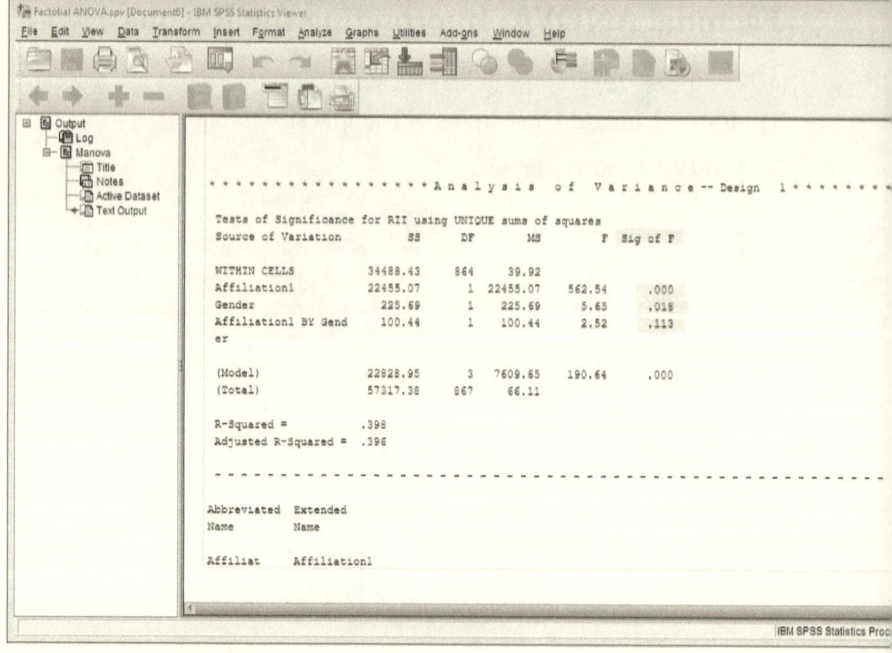

```
* * * * * * * * * * * * * * * * * * * * Analysis  of  Variance -- Design  1 * * * * * * * *

Tests of Significance for RII using UNIQUE sums of squares
Source of Variation         SS        DF        MS         F     Sig of F

WITHIN CELLS            34488.43      864      39.92
Affiliation1            22455.07        1   22455.07    562.54      .000
Gender                    225.69        1     225.69      5.65      .018
Affiliation1 BY Gend      100.44        1     100.44      2.52      .113
er

(Model)                 22828.95        3    7609.65    190.64      .000
(Total)                 57317.38      867      66.11

R-Squared =        .398
Adjusted R-Squared =   .396

- - - - - - - - - - - - - - - - - - - - - - - - - - - - - - - - - - - - -

Abbreviated  Extended
Name         Name

Affiliat     Affiliation1
```

The source table lists the sum of squares ('SS'), degrees of freedom ('df'), mean squares ('MS'), F statistic and its significance level. Remember that to determine if a main effect or the interaction is significant, we compare the 'Sig of F' to our decision rule ($\alpha=.01$).

If *Sig. of F* ≤ our decision rule ($\alpha=.01$) = significant F (Reject H$_0$)

If *Sig. of F* > our decision rule ($\alpha=.01$) = significant F (Fail to Reject H$_0$)

For the example above:

1) the interaction (*Affiliation1 BY Gender*) has a *Sig. of F (.113)* > .01, so the interaction is nonsignificant

2) the main effect for *Affiliation1* has a *Sig. of F (.001)* < .01, so this main effect is significant

3) the main effect for *Gender* has a *Sig. of F (.018)* > .01, so this main effect is nonsignificant - although it would be significant if we used a larger decision rule such as .05.

Just a couple of things you should notice about the numbers in the table. The source that is listed as *WITHIN CELLS* is the source of variation we generally call "error." Also, the source of variation listed as *(Model)* is calculated by adding up the sum of squares (SS) for the *Affiliation1* main effect plus the *Gender* main effect plus the interaction

(*Affiliation1 BY Gender*). "Model" is another way of saying overall treatment sum of squares. *(Total)* is all of the sums of squares added together: $34488.43 + 22455.07 + 225.69 + 100.44 = 57317.38$.

There are four F statistics listed in the output file. If we did not state a specific research hypothesis involving the main effects, then we first interpret the interaction term *(Affiliation1 BY Gender)*. If this is significant, then we would examine the design for simple main effects (or comparisons between treatment cells) using a multiple comparison test like LSD. If the interaction is significant that means that one factor moderates the effect that the other factor has on the dependent variable.

If the interaction is nonsignificant (as it is in the example), we examine both main effects (for *Affiliation1* and *Gender*). If either of these are significant, then we compare the group means (since there are only two levels of both of these factors) to determine which group scored higher on the RII scale.

In our example we wouldn't have to conduct multiple comparisons (for the significant main effect of *Gender*) because we only have two levels of that factor, so we know which levels are significantly different.

Factorial ANOVA: Reporting the Results

Research examining the interaction of gender and religious affiliation showed that those with a religious affiliation ($M = 30.48$, $SD = 5.5$) scored significantly higher of the RII scale than those who reported no religious affiliation ($M = 18.0$, $SD = 8.76$), $F_{(1,864)} = 562.54$, $MS_E = 39.92$, $p < .001$. The interaction was nonsignificant [$F_{(1,864)} = 2.52$, $MS_E = 39.92$, $p = .113$] and the main effect for gender was nearing significance [$F_{(1,864)} = 5.65$, $MS_E = 39.92$, $p = .018$], with males reporting slightly higher average RII scores than females.

Factorial ANOVA: Further Practice

You are a social psychologist researching the effect that cell phone use while driving (CELL) and gender of the driver has on the number of object struck while driving on a closed course (ERRORS). You decide to use a 2x2 between subjects factorial design. Gender (1=females; 2=males) and cell phone use (1 = cell phone use; 2 = no cell phone use) are thought to have an interaction effect on driving errors (0 = no errors; 100 = 100 objects struck).

SUBNUM	GENDER	CELL	ERRORS
1.00	1.00	1.00	75.00

2.00	1.00	1.00	76.00
3.00	1.00	1.00	91.00
4.00	1.00	1.00	78.00
5.00	1.00	1.00	84.00
6.00	1.00	1.00	70.00
7.00	1.00	1.00	80.00
8.00	1.00	1.00	96.00
9.00	1.00	1.00	77.00
10.00	1.00	1.00	81.00
11.00	1.00	2.00	53.00
12.00	1.00	2.00	51.00
13.00	1.00	2.00	46.00
14.00	1.00	2.00	63.00
15.00	1.00	2.00	58.00
16.00	1.00	2.00	57.00
17.00	1.00	2.00	43.00
18.00	1.00	2.00	51.00
19.00	1.00	2.00	54.00
20.00	1.00	2.00	61.00
21.00	2.00	1.00	52.00
22.00	2.00	1.00	49.00
23.00	2.00	1.00	39.00
24.00	2.00	1.00	38.00
25.00	2.00	1.00	44.00
26.00	2.00	1.00	49.00
27.00	2.00	1.00	47.00
28.00	2.00	1.00	57.00
29.00	2.00	1.00	48.00
30.00	2.00	1.00	53.00
31.00	2.00	2.00	44.00
32.00	2.00	2.00	54.00
33.00	2.00	2.00	34.00
34.00	2.00	2.00	53.00
35.00	2.00	2.00	49.00
36.00	2.00	2.00	48.00
37.00	2.00	2.00	50.00
38.00	2.00	2.00	41.00
39.00	2.00	2.00	54.00
40.00	2.00	2.00	48.00

Chapter 5: Repeated Measures Analysis of Variance (ANOVA)

Now consider a research design that involves the repeated measurement of the same sample of study participants over three or more measurement periods. These designs are called either within-subjects or repeated measures designs. Psychological science is eliminating the word "subjects," so we will use the more accurate name "repeated measures." For our example, we measured three dimensions of "religious practice" related to:

1) attending services (*RPServices*)
2) praying/mediating (*RPPray*)
3) reading scripture/important literature (*RPScripture*)

All where measured with similarly worded items and with the same scale responses. This analysis will determine if there is a significant difference between the three measures of religious practice across the sample.

Repeated Measures ANOVA: Step-By-Step

Step 1 (a) File; b) New; c) Syntax

Step 2: Type MANOVA command for factorial ANOVA

MANOVA *dvmeasure1 dvmeasure2 dvmeasure3*
    /WSFACTORS=repeatedmeasuresname (# levels)
    /PRINT SIGNIF (AVONLY)
    /OMEANS.

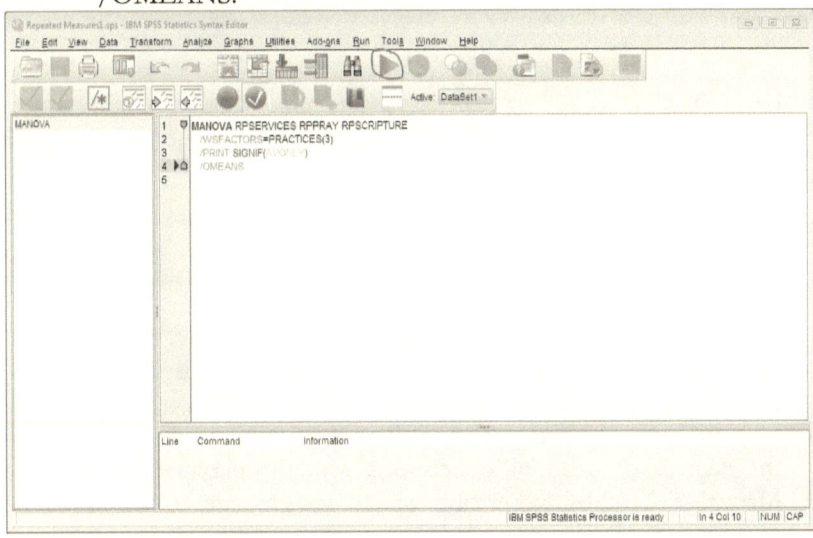

For the current example: dvmeasure1=*RPServices*; dvmeasure2=*RPPray*; dvmeasure3=*RPScripture*; WSFACTORS =*PRACTICES* (3)

There were three measurements of each person's level of religious practices related to attending services, praying and read scripture so those are listed as the three dependent variable measures. SPSS® requires us to give the collection of dependent variable measures a name (at the WSFACTORS subcommand), so we named it "Practices," since all three measures are related to religious practices. We also need to identify how many of the dependent variable measures list in the first line of the command are levels of the WSFACTOR we named. In our example, all three (3) measures listed are levels of the one and only repeated measure variable so we typed, "WSFACTORS=PRACTICES(3).

Repeated Measures ANOVA: Interpreting the Results

The output file for this analysis includes four tables.

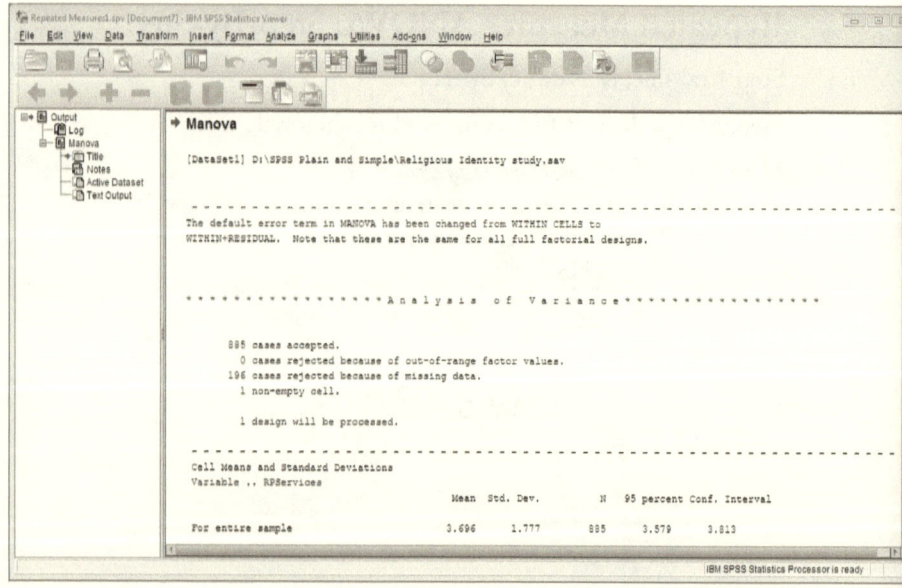

(1) Descriptive Statistics, which listed the means and standard deviations for each of the repeated measures levels; (2) Between-Subjects Tests, which we do NOT interpret. The only use of this table is for the WITHIN CELLS degrees of freedom that are equal to the degrees of freedom associations with the participants (df$_p$). (3) Mauchly's Test of Sphericity, which we evaluate to determine if

spherity can be assumed; and (4) Tests of Within-Subjects Effects that lists the results of our repeated measures ANOVA, under the assumption that sphericity has not been broken.

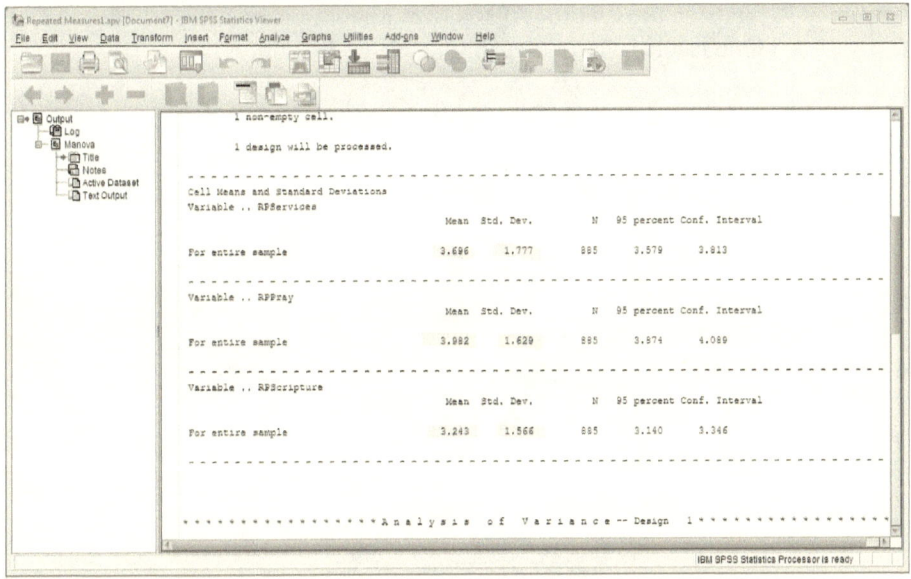

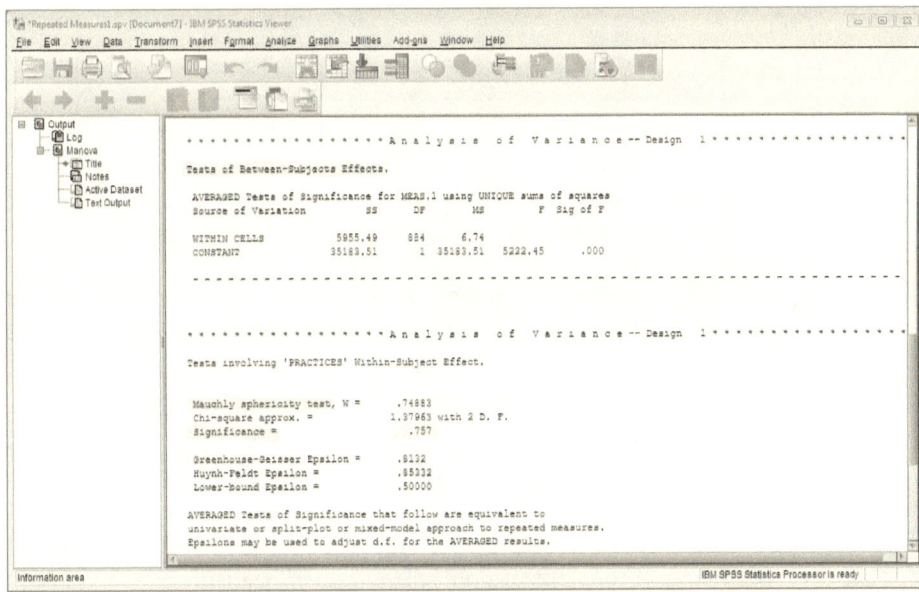

In order to interpret the output, we must first determine if we should assume sphericity or not by examining Mauchly's Test of Sphericity. Like all other statistics, we compare the significance level of the statistical test (reported under "Significance" in the Mauchly table) to our decision rule ($\alpha=.01$). In our study of three different religious practices, *we have not broken the assumption of sphericity* (Significance = .757 > α = .01). Since we can assume sphericity, we will evaluate the F statistic listed in the "Tests of Within-Subjects Effects" table, which immediately follows Mauchly's table in the output file.

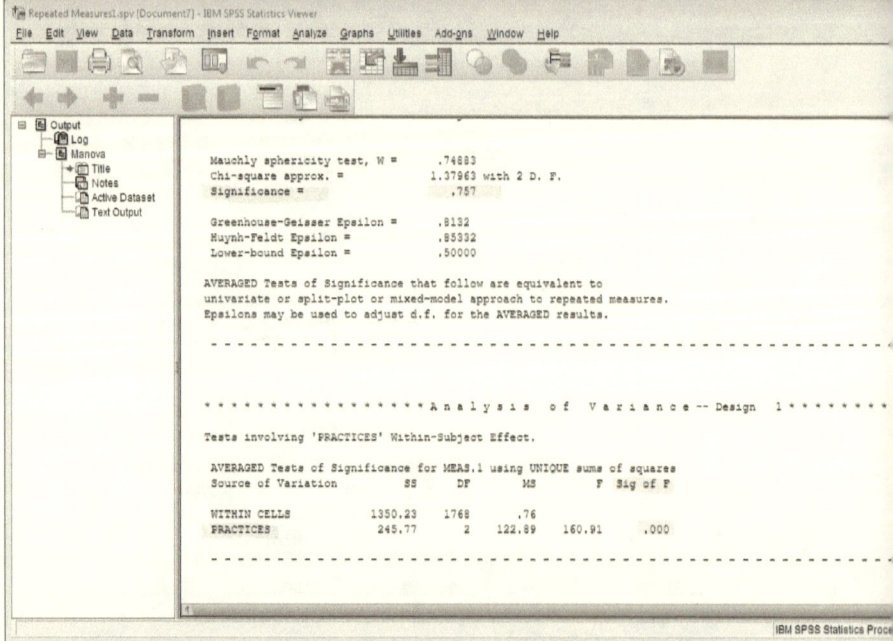

This ANOVA source table reports variance estimates for the two sources of variability in our design: (1) treatment (PRACTICES) and (2) error. In addition to the variance estimates (or mean squares) of treatment and error, the source table also lists the sums of squares, degrees of freedom (df), the F ratio (i.e., statistic), and the significance level (Sig.) of the F test. This F statistic is significant because the calculated significance level for the statistic is $p < .001$ which is less than our decision rule of $\alpha=.01$. The next step in the analysis would then be to conduct multiple comparison tests.

Let's examine how the numbers listed in the source table were calculated from the data. Remember that the F statistic, or sometime called the F ratio, is a ratio between variance due to the treatment conditions and variance due to error (unknown source(s) of variability). From the output then, our F statistic of 160.91 was calculated by dividing mean square treatment ($MS_{PRACTICES}=122.89$) by the mean square error, which is listed as "WITHIN CELLS" ($MS_{ERROR}=.76$). Working backward through the output, the mean squares were calculated by dividing the sums of squares by their respective degrees of freedom. So, the $MS_{PRACTICES}$=122.89 was calculated by dividing the $SS_{PRACTICES}$=245.77 by the $df_{PRACTICES}$=2. Likewise, the MS_{ERROR}=.76 was calculated by dividing the SS_{ERROR}=1350.23 by the df_{ERROR}=1765.

The Repeated Measures ANOVA command does not provide multiple comparison tests in the analysis. We must conduct these tests the old fashioned way, *by hand!* The formulae of most *post hoc* multiple comparison tests include the $\underline{MS}_{ERROR}$ and df_{ERROR} are listed on the "Within-Subjects Test" source table.

Repeated Measures ANOVA: Reporting the Results

In a study measuring three dimensions of religious practices, there was a significant difference among the three measures of attending services ($M = 3.7$, $SD = 1.78$), praying or mediating ($M = 3.98$, $SD = 1.63$) and reading scripture ($M = 3.24$, $SD = 1.57$) [F (2,1768) = 160.91, $MS_E = .76$, $p < .001$]. People reported engaging significantly more in prayer or attending services compared to reading their scripture/sacred texts.

Repeated Measures ANOVA: Further Practice

Now we are interested in examining the effects of taking a statistics course on math anxiety. We will measure math anxiety on a (0=no anxiety;10=extremely high anxiety) scale the first day of class, 4 weeks and 8 weeks into the semester. What do you conclude about the effects of taking a statistics course on the math anxiety of college students? Use Tukey's HSD for multiple comparisons and remember that you must conduct the multiple comparisons by hand. Remember that in SPSS® you must use variable names of 8 characters or less and that begin with a letter (try "FIRST," "WK4," "WK8").

STUDENT	FIRST DAY	4 WEEKS	8 WEEKS
1.00	5.00	5.00	6.00
2.00	3.00	4.00	3.00
3.00	3.00	3.00	6.00
4.00	4.00	4.00	3.00
5.00	5.00	5.00	4.00
6.00	5.00	5.00	4.00
7.00	4.00	5.00	5.00
8.00	2.00	5.00	5.00
9.00	4.00	2.00	7.00
10.00	5.00	4.00	6.00

11.00	3.00	7.00	4.00
12.00	3.00	5.00	4.00
13.00	6.00	3.00	6.00
14.00	3.00	4.00	4.00
15.00	6.00	6.00	6.00
16.00	2.00	3.00	3.00
17.00	5.00	2.00	5.00
18.00	4.00	3.00	2.00
19.00	6.00	6.00	6.00
20.00	4.00	6.00	5.00
21.00	4.00	5.00	4.00
22.00	3.00	3.00	4.00
23.00	3.00	6.00	5.00
24.00	5.00	4.00	3.00
25.00	2.00	5.00	6.00
26.00	5.00	3.00	5.00
27.00	5.00	3.00	4.00
28.00	3.00	4.00	4.00
29.00	5.00	6.00	4.00
30.00	5.00	2.00	3.00

Chapter 6: Split-Plot Analysis of Variance (ANOVA)

Split-Plot ANOVA: Step-by-Step

Step 1 (a) File; b) New; c) Syntax

Step 2: Type MANOVA command for factorial ANOVA

MANOVA *dvmeasure1 dvmeasure2* BY *betweensubjectsvariable (min, max)*
    /WSFACTORS=repeatedmeasuresname (# levels)
    /PRINT SIGNIF (AVONLY)
    /OMEANS.

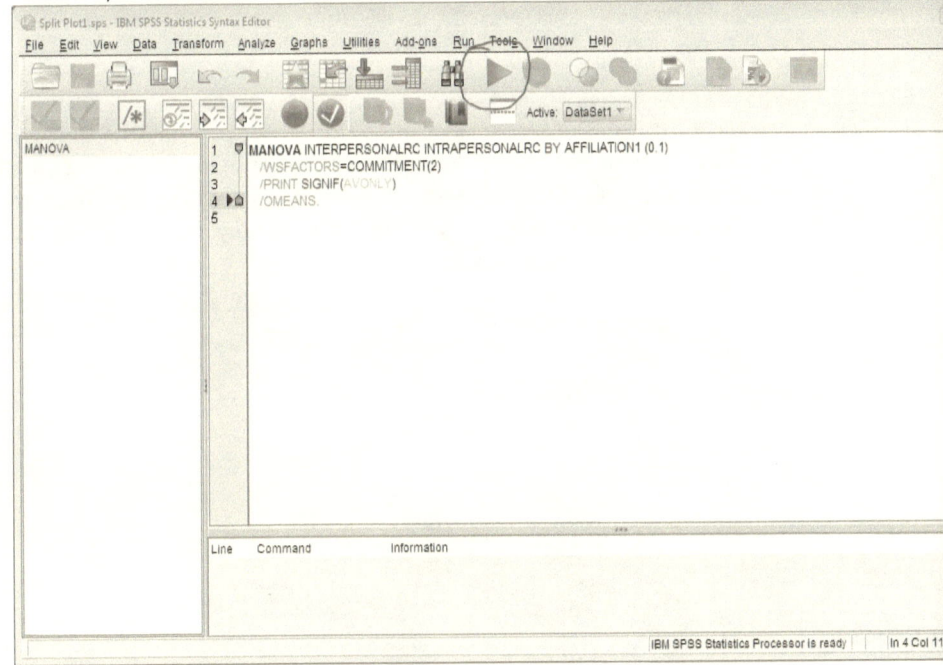

There are two dependent variable measurements in this example (*Interpersonal RC and Intrapersonal RC*) and one between-subjects factor (*Affiliation1*). *Affiliation1* has 2 levels that are coded 0 (minimum value) and 1 (maximum value). On the WSFACTORS subcommand we named the repeated measure variable *Commitment* because the two levels of this variable are interpersonal and intrapersonal religious commitment.

Split-Plot ANOVA: Interpreting the Results

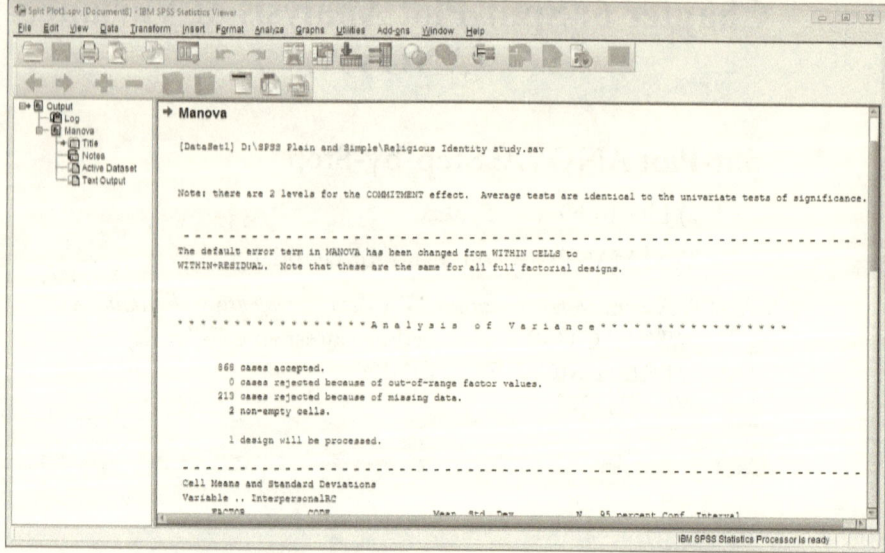

The first table in the output lists the descriptive statistics for each of our treatment cells. Of course, these descriptives are necessary for any multiple comparison tests as well as for reporting our results in an APA style research manuscript.

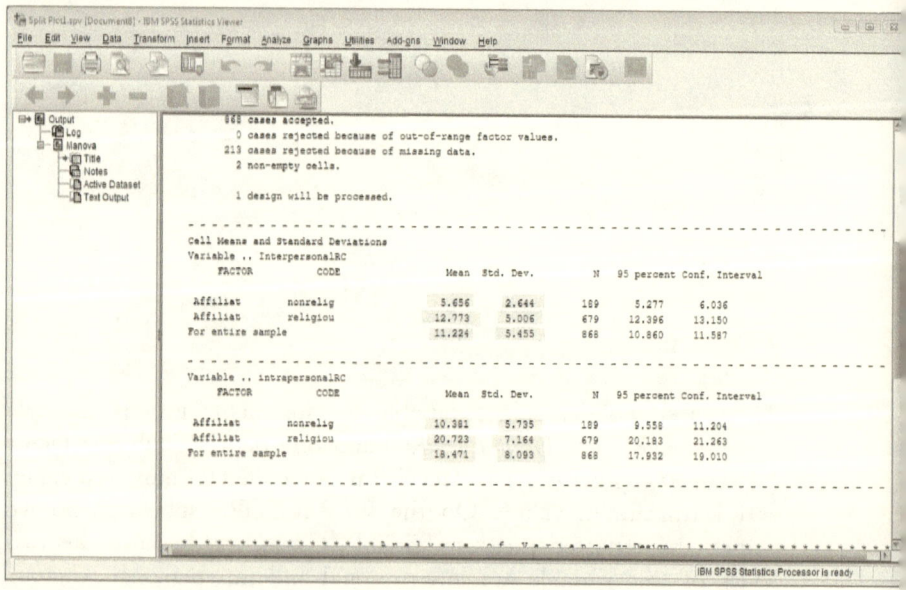

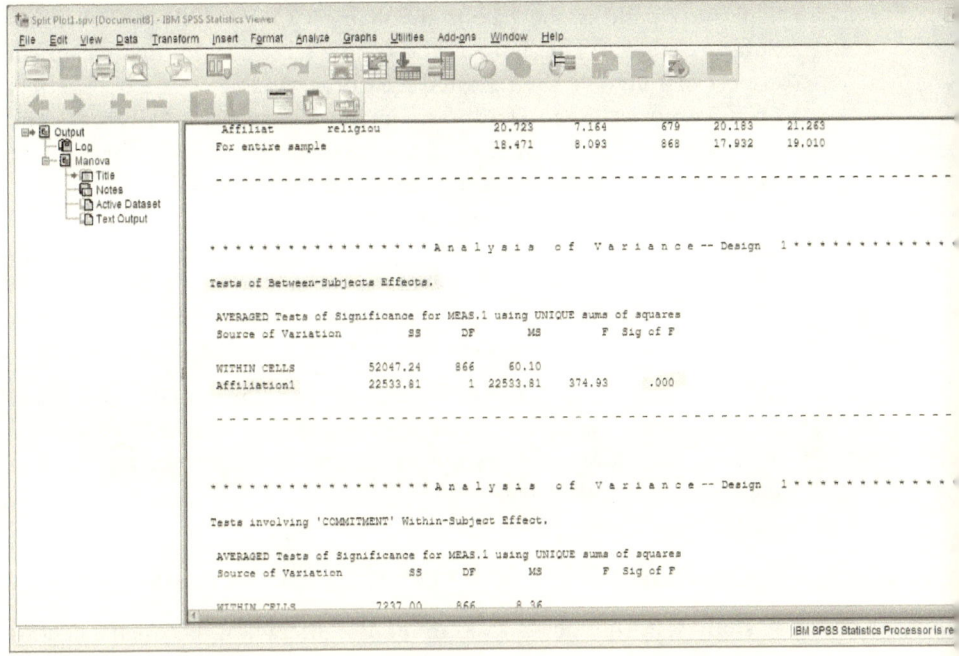

Split Plot1.spv [Document8] - IBM SPSS Statistics Viewer

File   Edit   View   Data   Transform   Insert   Format   Analyze   Graphs   Utilities   Add-ons   Window   Help

Output
  Log
  Manova
    Title
    Notes
    Active Dataset
    Text Output

```
        Affiliat    religiou              20.723    7.164    679    20.183    21.263
        For entire sample                 18.471    8.093    866    17.932    19.010

- - - - - - - - - - - - - - - - - - - - - - - - - - - - - - - - - - - - - - -


* * * * * * * * * * * * * * * * * * * * A n a l y s i s   o f   V a r i a n c e -- Design  1 * * * * * * * * * * * * * *

Tests of Between-Subjects Effects.

    AVERAGED Tests of Significance for MEAS.1 using UNIQUE sums of squares
    Source of Variation         SS       DF      MS        F   Sig of F


    WITHIN CELLS             52047.24    866    60.10
    Affiliation1             22533.81      1 22533.81   374.93     .000


- - - - - - - - - - - - - - - - - - - - - - - - - - - - - - - - - - - - - - -


* * * * * * * * * * * * * * * * * * * * A n a l y s i s   o f   V a r i a n c e -- Design  1 * * * * * * * * * * * * * *

Tests involving 'COMMITMENT' Within-Subject Effect.

    AVERAGED Tests of Significance for MEAS.1 using UNIQUE sums of squares
    Source of Variation         SS       DF      MS        F   Sig of F

    WITHIN CELLS              7237.00    866     8.36
```

IBM SPSS Statistics Processor is re

This table is the source table for the main effect of the between-subjects factor (*Affiliation1*). For the example, the main effect is statistically significant since the "Sig of F" is .001, which is less than .01. However, we almost always interpret the interaction first, so we will continue to look further down the output.

Split Plot1.spv [Document8] - IBM SPSS Statistics Viewer

File   Edit   View   Data   Transform   Insert   Format   Analyze   Graphs   Utilities   Add-ons   Window   Help

Output
  Log
  Manova
    Title
    Notes
    Active Dataset
    Text Output

```
        Source of Variation         SS       DF      MS        F   Sig of F

    WITHIN CELLS             52047.24    866    60.10
    Affiliation1             22533.81      1 22533.81   374.93     .000

- - - - - - - - - - - - - - - - - - - - - - - - - - - - - - - - - - - - - - -


* * * * * * * * * * * * * * * * * * * * A n a l y s i s   o f   V a r i a n c e -- Design  1 * * * * * * * * * * * * * *

Tests involving 'COMMITMENT' Within-Subject Effect.

    AVERAGED Tests of Significance for MEAS.1 using UNIQUE sums of squares
    Source of Variation         SS       DF      MS        F   Sig of F

    WITHIN CELLS              7237.00    866     8.36
    COMMITMENT               11875.82      1 11875.82  1421.10     .000
    Affiliation1 BY COMM       768.88      1   768.88    92.01     .000
    ITMENT

- - - - - - - - - - - - - - - - - - - - - - - - - - - - - - - - - - - - - - -


    Abbreviated  Extended
    Name         Name

    Affiliat     Affiliation1
```

IBM SPSS Statistics Processor is read

This next table is the "Tests involving 'COMMITMENT'" Within-Subjects effect." This table is the source table for the two treatment effects that involve the repeated measures variable: 1) the main effect of *Commitment* and 2) the interaction between *Affiliation1* and *Commitment*. We almost always interpret the interaction first, so we examine the "Affiliation1 BY Commitment" source of variation first. From the example, we see that the "Sig of F" is .001, so this interaction is significant. We also see that the main effect for *Commitment* is significant. However, since the interaction is significant, we would conduct multiple comparisons (e.g., LSD) on the 4 treatment cells lists in the descriptives table at the top of the output.

Make sure to use the correct degrees of freedom and MS_{ERROR} when calculating the multiple comparison tests. Those df and MS are listed in the same source table as the significant effect you are testing. For the example, the df = 866 and MS_{ERROR} = 8.36.

Split-Plot ANOVA: Reporting the Results

A study was conducted to examine the interaction between religious affiliation and two measures of religious commitment. A significant interaction was found [F (1, 866) = 92.01, MS_{ERROR} = 8.36, p < .001] with those categorized as "religious" having significantly higher intrapersonal religious commitment (M = 20.72, SD = 7.16) than interpersonal religious commitment (M = 12.77, SD = 5.01) or the intrapersonal religious commitment of those categorized as "nonreligious" (M = 10.38, SD = 5.74) All other comparisons were nonsignificant.

Split-Plot ANOVA: Further Practice

For additional practice conduct the split-plot ANOVA on the following data. Notice that this design is a 2 x 2 split-plot design.

This research question examines the effects of taking a statistics course on the insanity of students. We have a 2 (statistics course vs. history course) x 2 (pretest-posttest) split-plot design. We will measure sanity on a 0-10 scale with 0 representing being sane and 10 representing total insanity. The statistics course is coded 1 and the history course is coded as 2. What do you conclude about the effects of a statistics course on insanity using this split-plot design and measuring insanity before and after course completion? Write up the results in an APA style results section.

SUBNUM	CLASS	PRETEST	POSTTEST
1.00	1.00	4.00	2.00
2.00	1.00	6.00	3.00
3.00	1.00	4.00	4.00
4.00	1.00	5.00	7.00
5.00	1.00	4.00	4.00
6.00	1.00	6.00	5.00
7.00	1.00	5.00	5.00
8.00	1.00	7.00	4.00
9.00	1.00	5.00	6.00
10.00	1.00	6.00	5.00
11.00	1.00	4.00	2.00
12.00	1.00	5.00	4.00
13.00	1.00	4.00	4.00
14.00	1.00	7.00	6.00
15.00	1.00	5.00	3.00
16.00	2.00	9.00	2.00
17.00	2.00	8.00	3.00
18.00	2.00	7.00	6.00
19.00	2.00	8.00	5.00
20.00	2.00	7.00	3.00
21.00	2.00	8.00	6.00
22.00	2.00	8.00	4.00
23.00	2.00	9.00	3.00
24.00	2.00	9.00	2.00
25.00	2.00	6.00	5.00
26.00	2.00	8.00	6.00
27.00	2.00	10.00	5.00
28.00	2.00	9.00	6.00
29.00	2.00	8.00	4.00
30.00	2.00	8.00	3.00

Chapter 7: Bivariate Correlation and Linear Regression

Bivariate Correlation: Step-By-Step

Step 1:

a) Analyze

b) Correlate

c) Bivariate

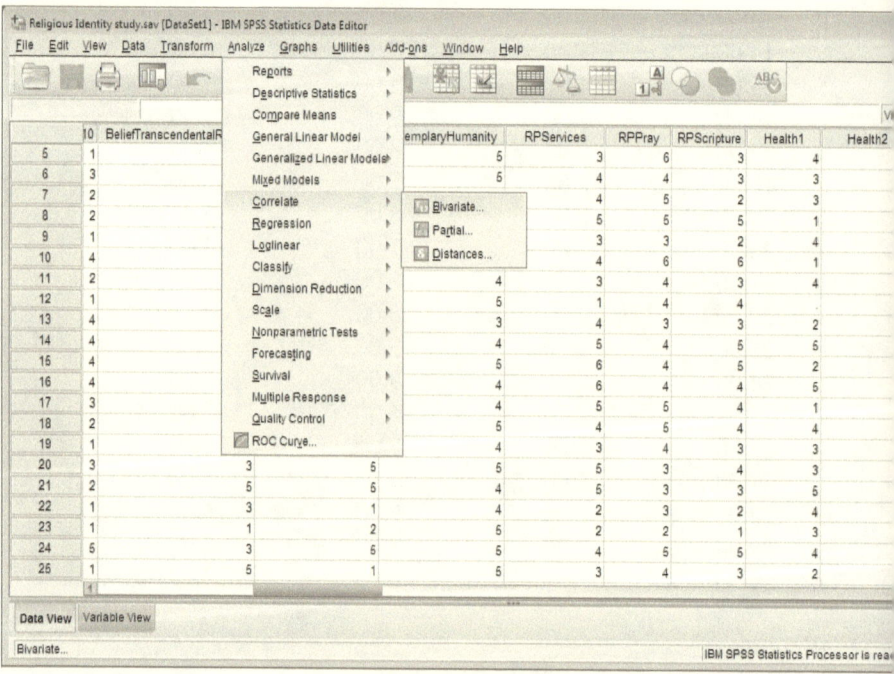

Step 2:

a) Select variables to correlate (all can be selected for the same analysis)

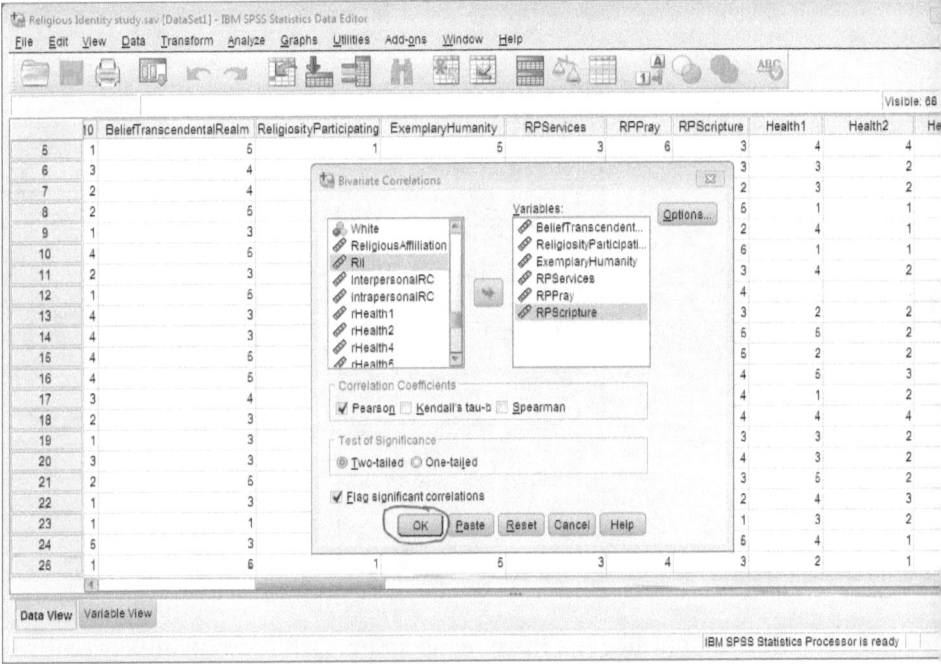

b) OK

Bivariate Correlation: Interpreting the Results

Birariate Correlation1.spv [Document9] - IBM SPSS Statistics Viewer

File   Edit   View   Data   Transform   Insert   Format   Analyze   Graphs   Utilities   Add-ons   Window   Help

Output
  Log
  Correlations
    Title
    Notes
    Active Dataset
    Correlations

➜ **Correlations**

[DataSet1] D:\SPSS Plain and Simple\Religious Identity study.sav

Correlations

		BeliefTranscendentalRealm	ReligiosityParticipating	ExemplaryHumanity	RPServices	RPPray	RPScripture
BeliefTranscendentalRealm	Pearson Correlation	1	.546**	.342**	.527**	.602**	.519**
	Sig. (2-tailed)		.000	.000	.000	.000	.000
	N	890	890	890	885	885	885
ReligiosityParticipating	Pearson Correlation	.546**	1	.297**	.805**	.599**	.645**
	Sig. (2-tailed)	.000		.000	.000	.000	.000
	N	890	890	890	885	885	885
ExemplaryHumanity	Pearson Correlation	.342**	.297**	1	.246**	.328**	.256**
	Sig. (2-tailed)	.000	.000		.000	.000	.000
	N	890	890	890	885	885	885
RPServices	Pearson Correlation	.527**	.805**	.246**	1	.682**	.749**
	Sig. (2-tailed)	.000	.000	.000		.000	.000
	N	885	885	885	885	885	885
RPPray	Pearson Correlation	.602**	.599**	.328**	.682**	1	.750**
	Sig. (2-tailed)	.000	.000	.000	.000		.000
	N	885	885	885	885	885	885
RPScripture	Pearson Correlation	.519**	.645**	.256**	.749**	.750**	1
	Sig. (2-tailed)	.000	.000	.000	.000	.000	
	N	885	885	885	885	885	885
RII	Pearson Correlation	.570**	.659**	.292**	.686**	.656**	.687**
	Sig. (2-tailed)	.000	.000	.000	.000	.000	.000
	N	890	890	890	885	885	885

IBM SPSS Statistics Proc

The output file lists three numbers for each correlation between two variables: 1) the Pearson r statistic; 2) the significance level; and 3) the sample size (N) of that correlation. In the example, the variables of *BeliefTranscendentalRealm* and *ReligiosityParticipating* are significantly related or correlated since "Sig (2-tailed) is less than .01 (our decision rule). The correlations has a positive value ($r = .546$) so that means that as the *Belief* variable increases in value, the *Religiosity* variable also increases in value (and visa versa). Remember that the correlation coefficient tells us two things about the relationship between the predictor variable and dependent variable. The sign of a *significant* coefficient tells us if the relationship is positive or negative. A positive relationship represents high values on the predictor variable *tend* to be associated with high values on the dependent variable and, likewise, low values on the predictor variable *tend* to be associated with low values on the dependent variable. A negative relationship represents that high values on the predictor variable *tend* to be associated with low values on the dependent variable and low values on the predictor variable *tend* to be associated with high values on the dependent variable. The value of a correlation coefficient is 0.00 to 1.00, where 0.00 represents no relationship between the variables and 1.00 represents a perfect relationship.

Linear Regression: Step-By-Step

Step1:

a) Analyze

b) Regression

c) Linear

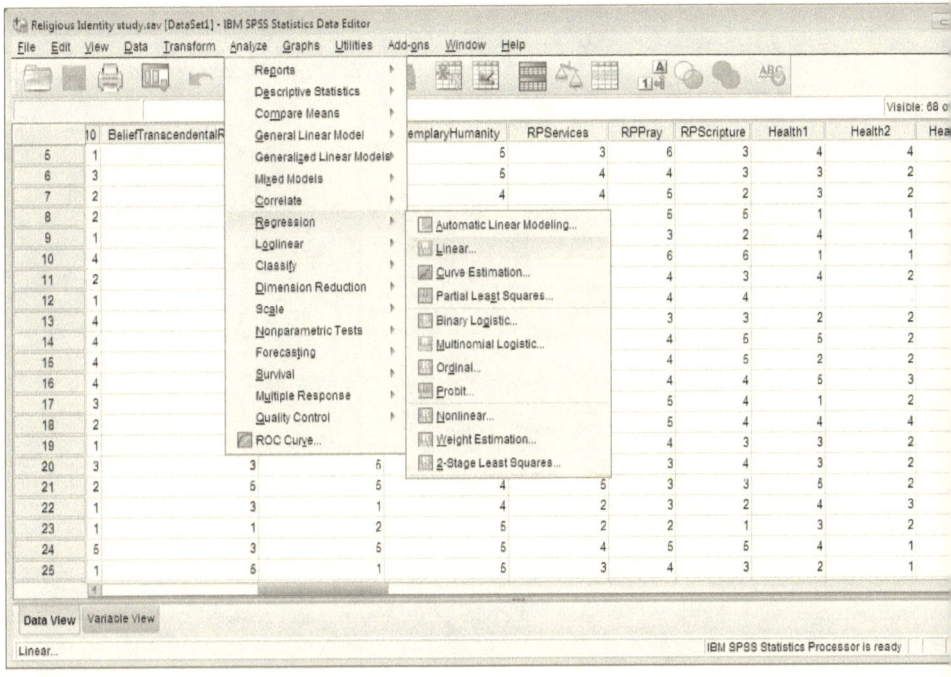

Step 2:

a) Select dependent variable

b) Select all of the predictors (independent variables) to be used in the regression analysis

c) Change the "Method" to Backward

d) OK

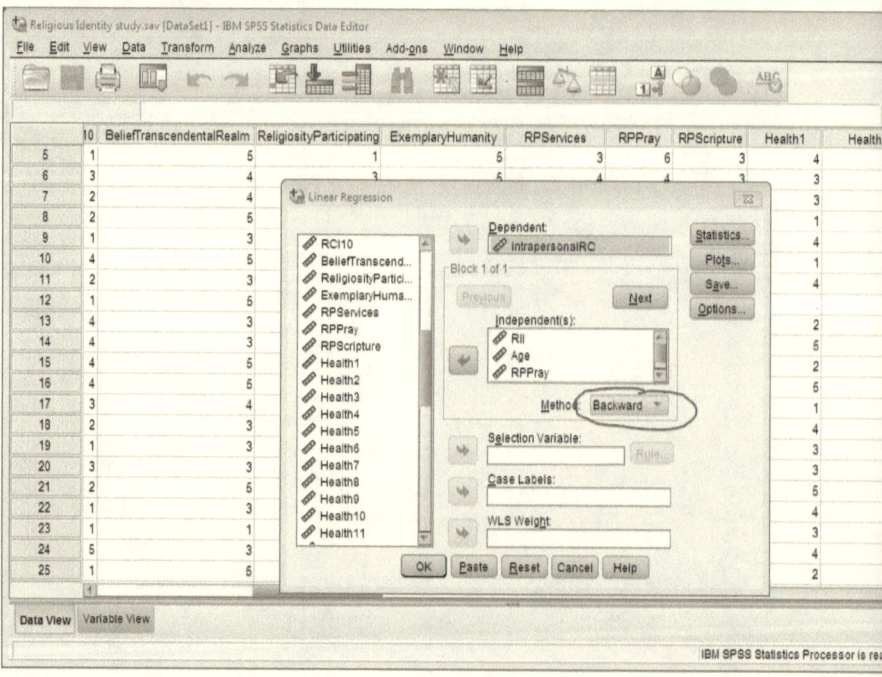

Linear Regression: Interpreting the Results

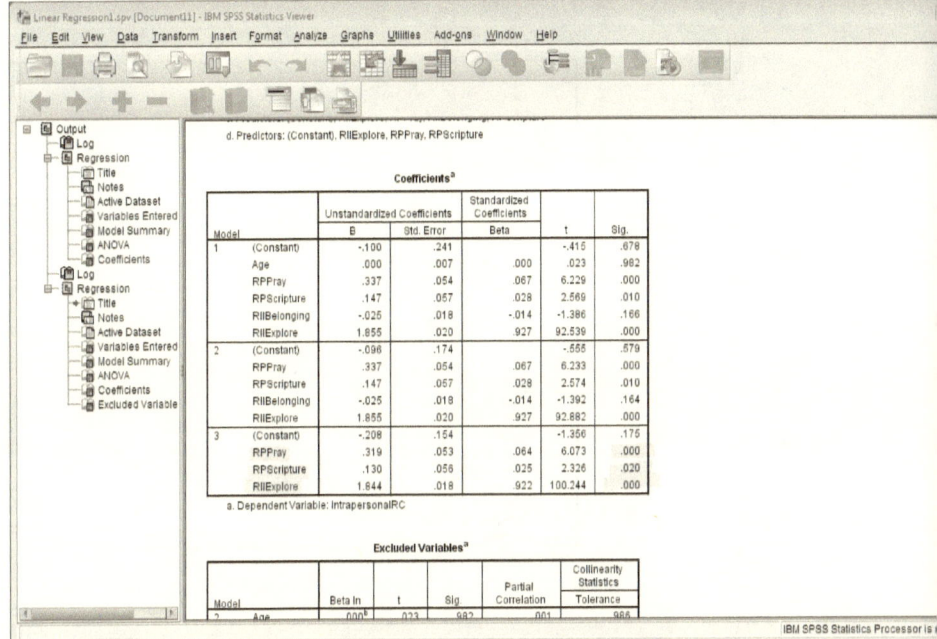

The output lists the predictor variables which are significantly related to the dependent variable in the last "Model" on the "Coefficients" table. In the example, there are three significant predictors: 1) *RPPray*; 2) *RPScripture*; and 3) *RIIExplore*.

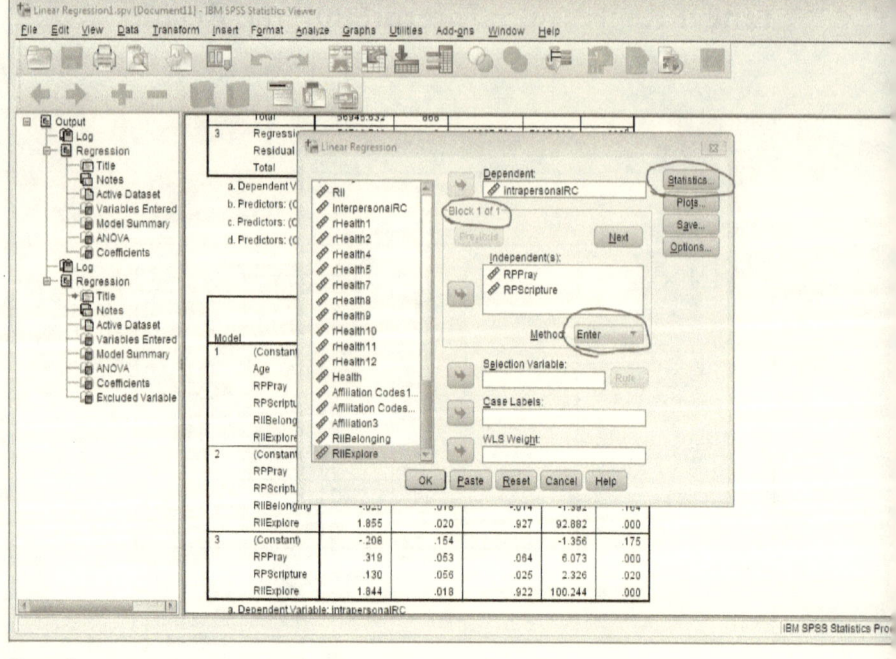

Step 2:

a) Again open the "Linear Regression" window (Analyze, Regression, Linear)

b) Select the dependent variable

c) Select all but **one** of the significant predictors (*RPPray* & *RPScripture*; *RIIExplore* is NOT selected yet)

d) Change the "Method" to "Enter"

e) Statistics

f) Select "R squared change"

g) Continue

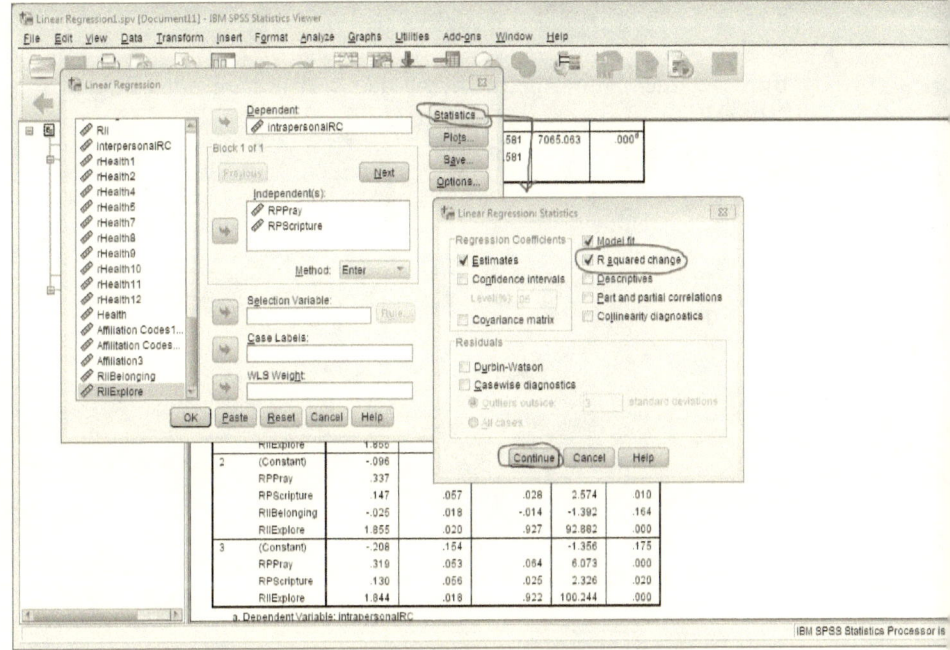

Step 3:

a) Next

b) Select the significant predictor that was not included in the first "Block"

c) Change "Method to "Enter"

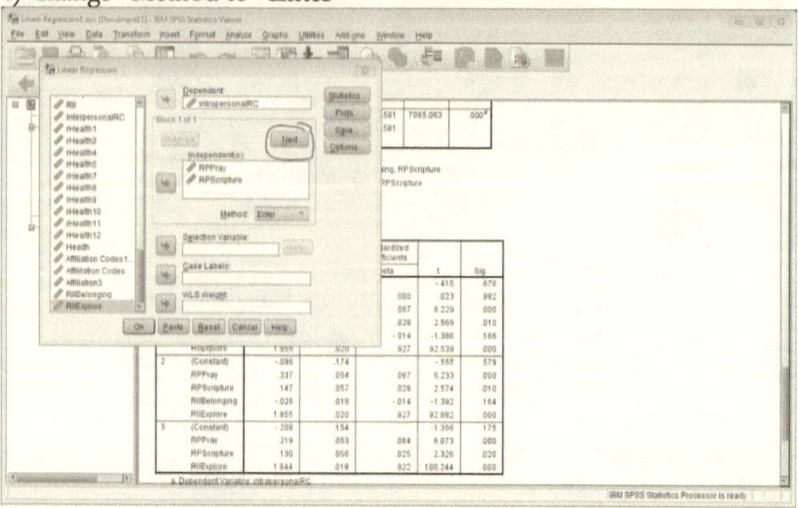

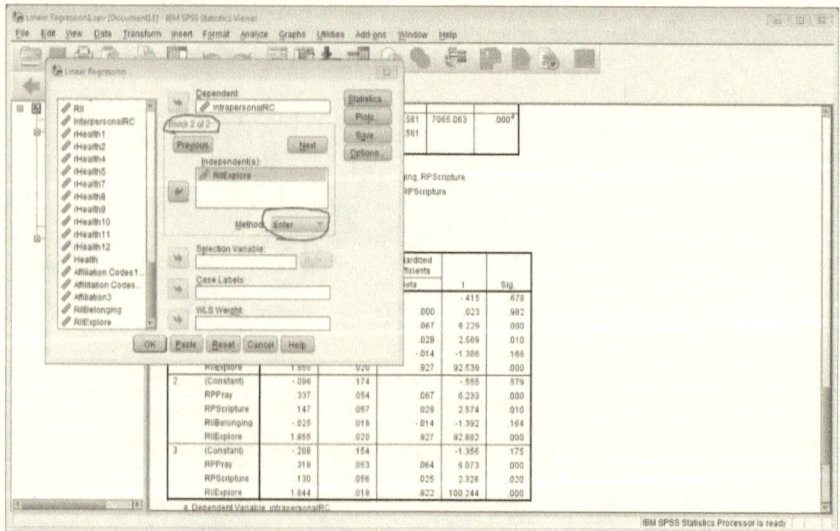

d) OK

Step 3:

a) Repeat Step 2 by selecting each significant predictor in the second "Block" after entering the other predictors (for the example, this Step would be conducted 3 times because there are 3 significant predictors)

Linear Regression: Interpreting the Results

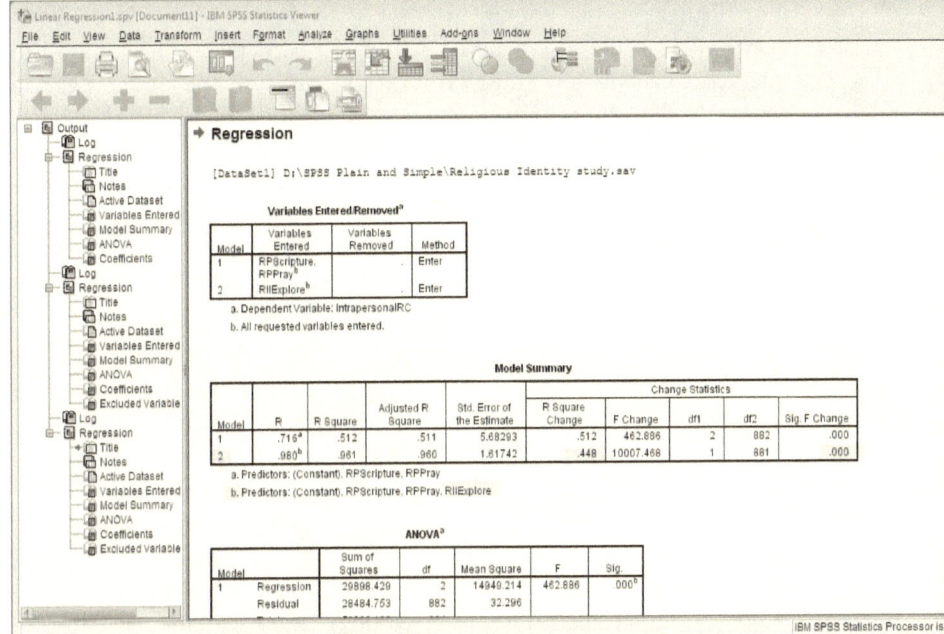

The "Model Summary" table calculate the percentage of *shared variance* (as called *explained variance* and *unique variance*). We convert the "R Square Change" value to a percentage, so the amount of shared variance between *IntrapersonalRC* (the dependent variable) and *RIIExplore* (the predictor variable entered in "Block 2 of 2" is 44.8%. We can think of this percentage as: "the percentage of a person's level of *IntrapersonalRC* by knowing their level of *RIIExplore*."

Linear Regression: Reporting the Results

[We actually report two pieces of information from the regression analysis: 1) the best prediction equation; which we develop from the "Coefficients" table of the "Backward" Method regression analysis conducted first. 2) the percentage of shard variance between each significant predictor and the dependent variable]

The regression analysis predicting intrapersonal religious commitment had the following best prediction equation: *IntrapersonalRC* = *RPPray* (.32) + *RPScripture* (.13) + *RIIExplore* (1.84) + (-.21).
         RIIExplore account for 44.8% unique variance in *IntrapersonalRC*.

[We then list the otehr two predictor variables unique variance based on the "Enter" Method regression analyses]

Linear Regression: Further Practice

For further practice you are attempting to predict scores on a driving test based on the following data from 60 participants. In addition to the road driving test (DRIVING), you measure the drivers' age in years (AGE), the number of years the have been driving (YEARS), and a written test over the rules of the road (TEST). The driving score ranges from 0=poor driving to 20= great driving; age ranges from 16 to 75; years range from 0 to 25 years; and written test scores range from 0% to 100%. Analyze the following data using the linear regression procedure and write up the results in an APA style Results section. Make sure to report the best prediction model.

SUBNUM	DRIVING	AGE	YEARS	TEST
1.00	10.00	53.00	4.00	18.00
2.00	10.00	53.00	15.00	12.00
3.00	11.00	55.00	14.00	32.00
4.00	9.00	51.00	5.00	8.00
5.00	7.00	21.00	3.00	2.00
6.00	6.00	43.00	13.00	2.00
7.00	9.00	61.00	19.00	20.00
8.00	9.00	64.00	24.00	3.00
9.00	8.00	26.00	22.00	9.00
10.00	10.00	32.00	6.00	25.00
11.00	9.00	40.00	16.00	9.00
12.00	8.00	68.00	3.00	9.00
13.00	6.00	31.00	6.00	.00
14.00	13.00	45.00	1.00	32.00
15.00	8.00	54.00	24.00	6.00
16.00	9.00	57.00	12.00	5.00
17.00	6.00	39.00	10.00	.00
18.00	10.00	45.00	20.00	30.00
19.00	8.00	57.00	5.00	.00
20.00	10.00	59.00	17.00	6.00
21.00	6.00	22.00	14.00	.00
22.00	9.00	32.00	16.00	14.00
23.00	6.00	64.00	6.00	.00
24.00	8.00	29.00	24.00	18.00
25.00	10.00	38.00	12.00	15.00
26.00	10.00	44.00	15.00	19.00
27.00	11.00	42.00	9.00	34.00
28.00	10.00	68.00	21.00	12.00
29.00	8.00	70.00	18.00	.00
30.00	10.00	45.00	15.00	26.00
31.00	8.00	54.00	4.00	9.00

32.00	13.00	55.00	7.00	45.00
33.00	13.00	56.00	23.00	31.00
34.00	9.00	19.00	14.00	3.00
35.00	10.00	55.00	4.00	4.00
36.00	7.00	67.00	.00	.00
37.00	8.00	54.00	.00	.00
38.00	7.00	61.00	23.00	.00
39.00	10.00	67.00	7.00	17.00
40.00	12.00	39.00	2.00	39.00
41.00	10.00	64.00	9.00	23.00
42.00	7.00	28.00	9.00	9.00
43.00	10.00	69.00	23.00	8.00
44.00	11.00	41.00	16.00	35.00
45.00	6.00	45.00	12.00	8.00
46.00	10.00	20.00	17.00	3.00